Table Of Contents

Chapter 1: Understanding the Gut-Brain Connection

Introduction to the Gut-Brain Connection

Welcome to the fascinating world of the gut-brain connection! In this subchapter, we will explore how the gut and the brain are connected and how this connection can have a significant impact on children with Autism Spectrum Disorder (ASD) and Attention Deficit Hyperactivity Disorder (ADHD).

The gut-brain connection is a remarkable and complex relationship between our digestive system (the gut) and our brain. It involves a constant communication between the two, influencing not only our physical health but also our mental and emotional well-being.

For children with ASD and ADHD, understanding how the gut and brain interact is especially crucial. Research suggests that imbalances in the gut microbiome, which refers to the trillions of microorganisms living in our digestive system, can play a significant role in these conditions.

The gut microbiome is like a bustling city, teeming with different types of bacteria, viruses, and fungi. These microorganisms, collectively known as the gut flora, have a profound impact on our overall health. They help break down food, absorb nutrients, strengthen our immune system, and even produce neurotransmitters that affect our mood and behavior.

When the gut flora is imbalanced, it can lead to inflammation and affect the production of these neurotransmitters. This can contribute to symptoms commonly seen in children with ASD and ADHD, such as digestive issues, immune system dysfunction, anxiety, and difficulty with focus and attention.

Understanding this connection is empowering because it means that we can take steps to support and improve the gut health of children with ASD and ADHD. By making dietary changes, such as reducing processed foods and increasing the intake of fruits, vegetables, and probiotics, we can help restore balance in the gut microbiome.

Furthermore, addressing gut health can also positively impact behavior and cognitive function in these children. By promoting a healthy gut environment, we may see improvements in attention span, social interaction, language development, and overall well-being.

In the upcoming chapters, we will delve deeper into specific strategies and interventions that can help optimize the gut-brain connection for children with ASD and ADHD. We will explore the role of nutrition, gut-healing protocols, and lifestyle modifications that can make a significant difference in their lives.

So, get ready to embark on this exciting journey as we uncover the amazing gut-brain connection and discover how it can help children with Autism Spectrum Disorder and Attention Deficit Hyperactivity Disorder thrive and reach their full potential.

The Interplay between the Gut and the Brain

The gut-brain connection is a fascinating and essential aspect of our overall health and well-being. It refers to the close relationship between our digestive system (the gut) and our brain. This connection is especially important for children with Autism Spectrum Disorder (ASD) and Attention Deficit Hyperactivity Disorder (ADHD), as it can greatly impact their symptoms and overall quality of life.

Research has shown that there is a direct line of communication between the gut and the brain. This communication occurs through the vagus nerve, a long nerve that connects these two vital organs. Scientists have discovered that the gut is not only responsible for digestion but also plays a crucial role in regulating mood, behavior, and cognitive function.

For children with ASD, the gut-brain connection is particularly significant. Many studies have found a higher prevalence of gastrointestinal (GI) issues among individuals on the autism spectrum. These GI issues, such as constipation, diarrhea, and abdominal pain, can further worsen behavioral and cognitive symptoms in children with ASD. It is believed that an imbalance in the gut microbiota, the trillions of bacteria living in our digestive system, may be at the root of these GI problems.

Similarly, for children with ADHD, the gut-brain connection is a key area of investigation. Some studies have shown that children with ADHD may also experience higher rates of GI issues compared to neurotypical children. Although the exact mechanisms are still being explored, it is hypothesized that the gut microbiota may influence attention, impulsivity, and hyperactivity in children with ADHD.

Understanding the interplay between the gut and the brain opens up new possibilities for treatment and intervention. Researchers have found that certain dietary and lifestyle changes can positively influence the gut microbiota and subsequently improve symptoms in children with ASD and ADHD. These changes may include a diet rich in fiber, fruits, and vegetables, as well as the avoidance of certain processed foods and additives.

Additionally, probiotics, which are beneficial bacteria, have shown promise in improving gut health and reducing behavioral symptoms in children with ASD and ADHD. By restoring the balance of the gut microbiota, probiotics can potentially alleviate GI issues and positively impact cognitive and behavioral functioning.

In conclusion, the gut-brain connection is a vital area of study for children with ASD and ADHD. By understanding and nurturing this connection through dietary and lifestyle changes, we can potentially improve the overall well-being and quality of life for these children. Further research in this field is crucial to developing targeted interventions that harness the power of the gut-brain connection in helping children with ASD and ADHD thrive.

Significance of the Gut-Brain Connection in Autism and ADHD

The gut-brain connection is a fascinating and essential aspect of our overall health and well-being. It refers to the intricate relationship between our gut, or digestive system, and our brain. This connection plays a crucial role in the development and management of various conditions, including Autism Spectrum Disorder (ASD) and Attention Deficit Hyperactivity Disorder (ADHD).

For children with Autism and ADHD, understanding the significance of the gut-brain connection can be life-changing. Research has shown that there is a direct link between the health of our gut and the functioning of our brain. In fact, the gut is often referred to as our "second brain" because it contains millions of neurons that communicate with the brain through a network of nerves.

When the gut is not functioning properly, it can have a profound impact on our overall health and cognitive function. Many children with Autism and ADHD experience gastrointestinal issues such as constipation, diarrhea, and food sensitivities. These gut problems can lead to inflammation, which in turn affects the brain's ability to function optimally.

By addressing and improving the health of the gut, we can positively impact the symptoms of Autism and ADHD. Research has shown that dietary interventions, such as eliminating certain foods or incorporating gut-friendly foods, can lead to significant improvements in behavior, attention, and overall well-being.

Furthermore, the gut-brain connection also plays a crucial role in the production and regulation of neurotransmitters, which are chemicals that help transmit signals in the brain. Neurotransmitters like serotonin and dopamine are essential for regulating mood, behavior, and attention. Imbalances in these neurotransmitters have been linked to Autism and ADHD.

By supporting the gut-brain connection through proper nutrition and lifestyle choices, we can improve neurotransmitter balance and enhance cognitive function in children with Autism and ADHD. This can lead to reduced hyperactivity, improved focus, and better overall behavior.

In conclusion, the gut-brain connection holds immense significance for children with Autism and ADHD. Understanding and nurturing this connection through proper nutrition and lifestyle choices can lead to remarkable improvements in their overall well-being and cognitive function. By addressing gut health, we can empower children with Autism and ADHD to reach their full potential and lead fulfilling lives.

Unraveling Autism Spectrum Disorder (ASD)

Welcome to the subchapter on "Unraveling Autism Spectrum Disorder (ASD)" in the book "The Amazing Gut-Brain Connection: How it Helps Kids with Autism and ADHD." If you are a child with ADHD or Autism Spectrum Disorder (ASD), this section is specifically designed for you.

Autism Spectrum Disorder (ASD) is a condition that affects the way a person's brain works, making it harder for them to communicate and interact with others. It can also lead to repetitive behaviors and difficulty with social skills. However, recent research has shown that there is a strong connection between the gut and the brain, which can have a significant impact on kids with ASD.

The gut-brain connection refers to the communication network between your brain and your digestive system. Did you know that your gut contains millions of neurons, just like your brain? These neurons are constantly sending signals to your brain, influencing your thoughts, emotions, and behaviors.

For kids with ASD, this connection is even more critical. Studies have found that children with ASD often have imbalances in their gut bacteria and digestive issues, which can affect their brain health and overall well-being. By understanding and nurturing this gut-brain connection, we can help improve the symptoms of ASD and ADHD.

One way to support the gut-brain connection is through a healthy diet. Foods rich in fiber, such as fruits, vegetables, and whole grains, can promote good gut health and improve brain function. Probiotics, which are beneficial bacteria, can also be helpful in maintaining a balanced gut microbiome.

In addition to diet, managing stress levels is crucial. Stress can disrupt the gut-brain connection and worsen the symptoms of ASD and ADHD. Engaging in activities that you enjoy, such as playing sports, drawing, or listening to music, can help reduce stress and improve your overall well-being.

Furthermore, it is essential to remember that every child with ASD is unique, and what works for one may not work for another. It's important to work closely with healthcare professionals and your parents to find the best strategies and treatments for you.

In conclusion, understanding the gut-brain connection is crucial for children with Autism Spectrum Disorder (ASD) and ADHD. By focusing on a healthy diet, managing stress levels, and seeking professional guidance, we can unravel the mysteries of ASD and find ways to improve your daily life. Remember, you are not alone on this journey, and together we can navigate the challenges and unlock your incredible potential.

Definition and Diagnostic Criteria of Autism Spectrum Disorder

Autism Spectrum Disorder (ASD) is a neurodevelopmental disorder that affects children's social interaction, communication, and behavior. It is characterized by a wide range of symptoms and can vary in severity from mild to severe. This subchapter aims to provide a comprehensive understanding of the definition and diagnostic criteria of ASD, helping children with ADHD Autism and their families to better comprehend their condition.

ASD is a spectrum disorder, which means that it encompasses a range of conditions that may present differently in each individual. Some children with ASD may have difficulty with social interaction, such as making eye contact, understanding nonverbal cues, or developing and maintaining relationships. Others may have challenges in verbal and nonverbal communication, such as delayed speech development, repetitive language patterns, or difficulty understanding sarcasm or metaphors.

In addition to social and communication difficulties, children with ASD often display repetitive and restricted behaviors or interests. They may have intense focus on specific objects or topics, engage in repetitive movements like hand flapping or rocking, or become upset by changes in routine.

Diagnosing ASD requires a careful evaluation by healthcare professionals, including developmental pediatricians, psychologists, or psychiatrists. The Diagnostic and Statistical Manual of Mental Disorders (DSM-5) provides specific criteria for diagnosing ASD, including persistent deficits in social communication and interaction, as well as restricted and repetitive patterns of behavior, interests, or activities. The symptoms must be present in early childhood and significantly impact the child's daily functioning.

It is important to note that the diagnosis of ASD is not solely based on observable behaviors. Healthcare professionals also consider the child's developmental history, medical evaluations, and input from parents and caregivers. Early intervention and diagnosis are crucial for children with ASD, as it allows for the implementation of appropriate therapies and support strategies to maximize their potential and well-being.

Understanding the definition and diagnostic criteria of ASD helps children with ADHD Autism and their families to better navigate their journey. By identifying and acknowledging their unique challenges, they can seek the necessary support and interventions. The Gut-Brain Connection plays a significant role in the management of ASD, as it highlights the relationship between the gut microbiome and brain function. Exploring this connection can provide valuable insights into the development of targeted treatments and interventions that may assist children with ASD in achieving their full potential.

Prevalence and Impact of Autism Spectrum Disorder

The prevalence and impact of Autism Spectrum Disorder (ASD) is a significant topic that needs to be discussed in-depth. In this subchapter, we will explore the crucial aspects of ASD, focusing on how the gut-brain connection plays a vital role in children with autism and ADHD.

ASD is a neurodevelopmental disorder that affects communication, social interaction, and behavior. It is estimated that approximately 1 in 54 children in the United States are diagnosed with ASD, making it prevalent among the population. Children with ASD often face challenges in various areas, including academic performance, social relationships, and emotional well-being.

The gut-brain connection refers to the intricate communication system between the gut and the brain. This connection plays a crucial role in regulating various bodily functions, including digestion, metabolism, and even cognitive processes. Recent research has shown that children with ASD have a disrupted gut-brain connection, leading to imbalances in the gut microbiota and inflammation in the gut.

Understanding the gut-brain connection is essential for children with ASD and ADHD because it provides insights into potential treatment options. Many studies have shown that interventions targeting the gut, such as dietary changes and probiotic supplementation, can significantly improve symptoms associated with ASD and ADHD.

For children with ASD, adopting a specific diet known as the gluten-free, casein-free (GFCF) diet has shown promising results. This diet eliminates gluten (found in wheat) and casein (found in dairy products) as these proteins have been found to exacerbate symptoms in some individuals with ASD. Additionally, incorporating probiotics, which are beneficial bacteria, can help restore the balance of gut microbiota, reducing inflammation and improving overall gut health.

By understanding the gut-brain connection, children with ASD and ADHD can gain valuable insights into how their dietary choices and gut health can impact their overall well-being. It empowers them to make informed decisions about their health and explore potential treatment options that may alleviate their symptoms.

In conclusion, the prevalence and impact of Autism Spectrum Disorder are significant concerns for children with ASD and ADHD. Exploring the gut-brain connection provides valuable insights into potential treatment options that can improve their overall well-being. By adopting specific dietary changes and incorporating probiotics, children can regain balance in their gut microbiota, reducing inflammation and improving symptoms associated with ASD and ADHD.

Gut-Brain Connection in Children with Autism Spectrum Disorder

The gut-brain connection is a fascinating and important aspect of understanding the challenges faced by children with Autism Spectrum Disorder (ASD). In recent years, research has shown a strong link between the health of the gut and the functioning of the brain, particularly in individuals with ASD. This subchapter aims to shed light on this connection and explain how it can help children with Autism and ADHD.

Children with ASD often experience gastrointestinal issues such as constipation, diarrhea, and food sensitivities. These digestive problems can have a direct impact on their behavior, mood, and cognitive abilities. The gut is home to trillions of bacteria, collectively known as the gut microbiome, which play a crucial role in digestion, immune function, and brain development. When the balance of these bacteria is disrupted, it can lead to inflammation and other issues that affect the brain.

Scientific studies have revealed that children with ASD have a different composition of gut bacteria compared to their neurotypical peers. This imbalance, known as dysbiosis, can influence the production of neurotransmitters and other chemicals that regulate mood, cognition, and behavior. By understanding this connection, parents and healthcare professionals can explore interventions that target the gut microbiome to improve the symptoms of ASD.

One such intervention is the use of probiotics, which are beneficial bacteria that can help restore a healthy balance in the gut. Research has shown that certain strains of probiotics can reduce gastrointestinal symptoms and improve social communication and behavior in children with ASD. Additionally, dietary changes such as eliminating gluten and casein, which are proteins found in wheat and dairy products, have been found to alleviate symptoms in some individuals.

Understanding the gut-brain connection can also benefit children with Attention Deficit Hyperactivity Disorder (ADHD), as many of the same principles apply. Research has shown that children with ADHD often have gut dysbiosis and gastrointestinal symptoms similar to those seen in children with ASD. By addressing gut health, it is possible to improve attention, focus, and impulsivity in children with ADHD.

In conclusion, the gut-brain connection is a crucial area to explore when seeking to improve the lives of children with Autism Spectrum Disorder and ADHD. By understanding the influence of the gut on the brain, parents and healthcare professionals can implement targeted interventions to support these children's health and development. Whether through probiotics, dietary changes, or other approaches, optimizing the gut-brain connection holds great promise for improving the well-being of children with Autism and ADHD.

Decoding Attention Deficit Hyperactivity Disorder (ADHD)

Attention Deficit Hyperactivity Disorder (ADHD) is a neurodevelopmental disorder that affects many children worldwide. It is characterized by difficulties in paying attention, impulsivity, and hyperactivity. In this subchapter, we will delve into the intricacies of ADHD, how it affects children, and how the gut-brain connection plays a crucial role in managing this condition.

For children with ADHD, their brains work differently, making it challenging for them to concentrate and control their impulses. They may find it difficult to sit still, follow instructions, and complete tasks. This can lead to academic struggles, social challenges, and low self-esteem. However, understanding the gut-brain connection can provide valuable insights into managing the symptoms of ADHD.

The gut-brain connection refers to the bidirectional communication between the gut and the brain. The gut, also known as the second brain, contains millions of neurons that produce various neurotransmitters, including serotonin and dopamine, which are crucial for mood regulation and attention. Research has shown that imbalances in gut bacteria, inflammation in the gut, and leaky gut syndrome can contribute to the development and exacerbation of ADHD symptoms.

By addressing gut health, we can positively impact the symptoms of ADHD. Introducing a balanced diet rich in whole foods, fiber, and probiotics can promote a healthy gut microbiome. Studies have shown that certain probiotic strains, such as Lactobacillus and Bifidobacterium, can improve attention, reduce hyperactivity, and enhance cognitive function in children with ADHD.

Furthermore, eliminating food sensitivities and additives from the diet can also have a significant impact on ADHD symptoms. Certain foods, such as artificial colors, preservatives, and refined sugars, have been linked to increased hyperactivity and impulsivity. Identifying and removing these triggers can lead to improved focus and behavior.

In addition to dietary interventions, incorporating lifestyle changes can also benefit children with ADHD. Regular exercise, sufficient sleep, and stress reduction techniques, such as mindfulness and relaxation exercises, can help regulate neurotransmitter levels and promote overall well-being.

In conclusion, understanding the gut-brain connection is crucial for children with ADHD. By addressing gut health through dietary and lifestyle interventions, we can positively impact their symptoms and improve their quality of life. This subchapter serves as a guide for children with ADHD, providing them with valuable information and tools to navigate their condition and thrive.

Understanding Attention Deficit Hyperactivity Disorder

Attention Deficit Hyperactivity Disorder (ADHD) is a neurodevelopmental disorder that affects children and often persists into adulthood. It is characterized by difficulties in paying attention, impulsivity, and hyperactivity. ADHD is one of the most common childhood disorders, affecting approximately 8-10% of children worldwide.

Children with ADHD often struggle with staying focused on tasks, following instructions, and sitting still for extended periods. They may have trouble organizing their thoughts and belongings, leading to a disorganized and chaotic lifestyle. Additionally, impulsive behavior and difficulty controlling emotions are common in children with ADHD.

The gut-brain connection plays a crucial role in understanding and managing ADHD. Recent research has shown that there is a strong link between the gut and the brain, and disruptions in gut health can have a significant impact on mental health and neurodevelopmental disorders like ADHD.

The gut microbiome, a collection of trillions of bacteria living in our digestive system, has a profound influence on brain function. Studies have found that children with ADHD often have an imbalance in their gut microbiota, with a decrease in beneficial bacteria and an increase in harmful bacteria. This imbalance can lead to inflammation in the gut, which can then trigger inflammation in the brain, affecting cognitive function and behavior.

Understanding and addressing the gut-brain connection can be beneficial for children with ADHD. By focusing on improving gut health through diet, lifestyle changes, and targeted interventions, we can potentially reduce symptoms and improve overall well-being.

A healthy diet is crucial for maintaining a balanced gut microbiome. Avoiding processed foods, sugar, and artificial additives while adding more fruits, vegetables, whole grains, and probiotic-rich foods can support gut health. Regular exercise and adequate sleep also play a significant role in managing ADHD symptoms.

Furthermore, certain supplements and interventions can help restore gut balance and support brain health. Probiotics, omega-3 fatty acids, and certain vitamins and minerals have shown promise in improving symptoms of ADHD. However, it is essential to consult with a healthcare professional before starting any supplements or interventions.

In conclusion, understanding the gut-brain connection is essential for children with ADHD. By addressing gut health through diet, lifestyle changes, and targeted interventions, we can potentially alleviate symptoms and improve overall quality of life. By nurturing a healthy gut, we can support the development of a healthy brain, paving the way for a brighter future for children with ADHD.

Prevalence and Impact of ADHD

Attention-Deficit/Hyperactivity Disorder (ADHD) is a neurodevelopmental disorder that affects many children worldwide. It is characterized by difficulties in maintaining attention, impulsivity, and hyperactivity. In recent years, there has been a significant increase in the prevalence of ADHD, making it a growing concern for both parents and healthcare professionals.

According to recent studies, approximately 5-10% of children are diagnosed with ADHD. Boys are more likely to be diagnosed with this disorder than girls, with a ratio of about 3:1. The exact cause of ADHD remains unknown; however, research suggests that it is a complex interplay of genetic and environmental factors.

The impact of ADHD on children's lives can be significant. Many children with ADHD struggle academically, as they find it challenging to concentrate and complete tasks. They may have difficulty following instructions, organizing their work, and staying on track. These academic struggles can lead to low self-esteem and frustration.

ADHD also affects social interactions and relationships. Children with ADHD often have difficulty controlling their impulses, leading to impulsive behavior and difficulty in social situations. They may interrupt others, struggle with turn-taking, and have trouble understanding social cues. These challenges can make it hard for them to form and maintain friendships, leading to feelings of isolation and loneliness.

The gut-brain connection plays a vital role in understanding the prevalence and impact of ADHD. Research suggests that there is a link between the gut microbiome, the collection of bacteria in our digestive system, and brain health. Disruptions in the gut microbiome can affect neurotransmitter production and regulation, which in turn can impact mood, behavior, and cognitive function.

Understanding this connection opens up new possibilities for managing ADHD symptoms. By focusing on gut health, children with ADHD can potentially experience improvements in attention, behavior, and overall well-being. Interventions such as dietary changes, probiotics, and other gut-supporting strategies have shown promising results in reducing ADHD symptoms.

In conclusion, ADHD is a prevalent neurodevelopmental disorder that affects many children worldwide. It has a significant impact on various aspects of their lives, including academics and social interactions. Understanding the gut-brain connection and its role in ADHD opens up new possibilities for managing symptoms and improving overall well-being. By addressing gut health, children with ADHD can potentially experience positive changes in their cognitive function, behavior, and quality of life.

Gut-Brain Connection in Children with ADHD

Attention Deficit Hyperactivity Disorder (ADHD) is a neurodevelopmental disorder that affects millions of children worldwide. It is characterized by difficulties in paying attention, impulsive behavior, and hyperactivity. While the exact cause of ADHD is still not fully understood, recent research has shed light on the fascinating Gut-Brain Connection, which may play a significant role in the development and management of this condition.

The Gut-Brain Connection refers to the intricate communication network between the brain and the gut, also known as the gastrointestinal system. This connection is bidirectional, meaning that signals can travel from the gut to the brain and vice versa. Scientists have discovered that the gut and the brain are in constant communication through neurotransmitters, hormones, and the vagus nerve.

For children with ADHD, understanding the Gut-Brain Connection can be particularly beneficial. Studies have found that individuals with ADHD often have imbalances in their gut microbiome, which is the community of microorganisms living in the digestive tract. These imbalances can lead to inflammation and an increased permeability of the gut lining, known as leaky gut syndrome. When the gut lining becomes permeable, toxins and bacterial byproducts can enter the bloodstream and affect the brain, potentially exacerbating ADHD symptoms.

Moreover, the gut microbiome also produces various neurotransmitters, including serotonin and dopamine, which are crucial for regulating mood and attention. Imbalances in these neurotransmitters can contribute to the development and severity of ADHD symptoms. By focusing on improving gut health, children with ADHD may experience a reduction in symptoms and an overall improvement in their well-being.

There are several ways to support the Gut-Brain Connection for children with ADHD. A healthy diet rich in fruits, vegetables, whole grains, and lean proteins can provide essential nutrients and support a diverse gut microbiome. Probiotics, which are beneficial bacteria, may also be helpful in rebalancing the gut microbiome and reducing inflammation.

In addition to dietary changes, managing stress levels and getting enough sleep can positively impact the Gut-Brain Connection. Chronic stress can disrupt the gut microbiome and increase inflammation, while adequate sleep promotes a healthy balance of neurotransmitters.

While the Gut-Brain Connection is a relatively new field of study, emerging research suggests that it holds great potential in understanding and managing ADHD symptoms. By nurturing a healthy gut through diet, lifestyle choices, and possibly targeted interventions, children with ADHD can potentially experience improved focus, reduced hyperactivity, and a better overall quality of life.

Chapter 2: The Role of the Gut Microbiome

Introduction to the Gut Microbiome

Welcome to the fascinating world of the gut microbiome! In this chapter, we will dive into the incredible connection between your gut and brain, and how it can help children with Autism Spectrum Disorder (ASD) and Attention Deficit Hyperactivity Disorder (ADHD).

The gut microbiome refers to the trillions of bacteria, viruses, and other microorganisms that live in your digestive tract. These tiny creatures play a crucial role in maintaining your overall health and well-being. Believe it or not, they even have an impact on your brain!

For children with ASD and ADHD, understanding the gut-brain connection is particularly important. Research has shown that there is a strong link between gut health and these neurodevelopmental disorders. By taking care of your gut, you can potentially improve the symptoms associated with ASD and ADHD.

So how does the gut microbiome influence your brain? Well, it turns out that the microbes in your gut produce certain chemicals and metabolites that can communicate with your brain through a complex network of nerves and chemical messengers. This communication highway is known as the gut-brain axis.

When the balance of microbes in your gut is disrupted, it can lead to inflammation, which in turn can affect your brain's function. This inflammation has been linked to the symptoms of ASD and ADHD, such as difficulties with social interactions, attention problems, and sensory sensitivities.

The good news is that you have the power to improve your gut health and potentially reduce these symptoms! By making smart food choices and adopting a healthy lifestyle, you can nurture the beneficial bacteria in your gut and promote a balanced microbiome.

In the following chapters, we will explore various strategies and tips for optimizing your gut health. From incorporating probiotic-rich foods into your diet to managing stress levels, there are plenty of ways to support your gut-brain connection.

So get ready to embark on this exciting journey into the gut microbiome! By understanding how your gut and brain are intricately connected, you will gain valuable insights into managing your ASD or ADHD symptoms and improving your overall well-being. Let's dive in and discover the amazing world of the gut-brain connection together!

What is the Gut Microbiome?

The gut microbiome is a fascinating and complex system that plays a crucial role in the overall health and well-being of our bodies. But what exactly is it? Well, let's break it down!

The gut microbiome refers to the trillions of microorganisms that reside in our digestive tract, specifically in our intestines. These microorganisms include bacteria, viruses, fungi, and other microscopic organisms. It may sound strange to think that we have so many tiny creatures living inside of us, but they are actually incredibly beneficial!

These microorganisms in our gut microbiome have a symbiotic relationship with our bodies. In other words, we need them just as much as they need us. They help us break down and digest the food we eat, produce essential nutrients, and even regulate our immune system. But their importance doesn't stop there!

Recent research has shown a strong connection between the gut microbiome and conditions such as Autism Spectrum Disorder (ASD) and Attention Deficit Hyperactivity Disorder (ADHD). Scientists have discovered that children with ASD and ADHD often have an imbalance in their gut microbiome, with an overgrowth of harmful bacteria and a decrease in beneficial ones.

This imbalance can lead to a variety of symptoms, including gastrointestinal issues, inflammation, and even behavioral problems. It's believed that the communication between the gut and the brain, known as the gut-brain connection, plays a significant role in these conditions. When the gut microbiome is out of balance, it can send signals to the brain that affect mood, behavior, and cognitive function.

Understanding the gut microbiome and its connection to conditions like ASD and ADHD is incredibly important for children and their families. By addressing and rebalancing the gut microbiome, we can potentially alleviate some of the symptoms associated with these disorders.

In this book, "The Amazing Gut-Brain Connection: How it Helps Kids with Autism and ADHD," we will explore the fascinating world of the gut microbiome and its impact on the brain. We will delve into the latest research, provide practical tips and strategies for improving gut health, and showcase inspiring stories of children who have experienced positive changes through gut-brain connection therapies.

So, get ready to embark on an exciting journey through the gut-brain connection for kids with Autism Spectrum Disorder and ADHD. Together, we will uncover the amazing potential of the gut microbiome and how it can help us lead healthier, happier lives.

Importance of a Healthy Gut Microbiome

Subchapter: Importance of a Healthy Gut Microbiome

Introduction:
Welcome to this subchapter on the "Importance of a Healthy Gut Microbiome." In this section, we will explore how maintaining a healthy gut can have a positive impact on children with Autism Spectrum Disorder (ASD) and Attention-Deficit/Hyperactivity Disorder (ADHD). Understanding the gut-brain connection is crucial for improving the well-being and quality of life for children with these conditions.

The Gut-Brain Connection for Kids with Autism Spectrum Disorder:
Did you know that your gut plays a significant role in your brain's health? For children with Autism Spectrum Disorder, a healthy gut microbiome is particularly important. The gut is home to trillions of microorganisms, including bacteria, which form the gut microbiome. Research has shown that children with ASD often have imbalances in their gut microbiome, which can worsen their symptoms.

A healthy gut microbiome helps with digestion and supports the production of neurotransmitters, chemicals that communicate between the gut and the brain. When the gut microbiome is disturbed, it can lead to inflammation, affecting brain function and behavior. By taking care of your gut health through proper nutrition and lifestyle choices, you can positively impact your brain function and reduce the severity of ASD symptoms.

The Gut-Brain Connection for Kids with ADHD:
Attention-Deficit/Hyperactivity Disorder is another condition that can benefit from a healthy gut microbiome. Children with ADHD often experience difficulties with attention, hyperactivity, and impulsivity. Recent studies have shown a link between the gut microbiome and the symptoms of ADHD.

An imbalanced microbiome can increase inflammation in the body, which can affect brain function and worsen ADHD symptoms. By maintaining a healthy gut, children with ADHD may experience improved focus, reduced impulsivity, and better overall behavior. Incorporating a diet rich in fruits, vegetables, whole grains, and probiotic foods can promote a diverse and healthy gut microbiome.

Taking Care of Your Gut:

To promote a healthy gut microbiome, it is essential to adopt healthy habits. Start by incorporating a balanced diet with plenty of fiber-rich foods, such as fruits, vegetables, and whole grains. Limit the intake of processed foods, sugary snacks, and artificial additives, as these can disrupt the gut microbiome.

Regular exercise is also crucial for maintaining a healthy gut. Physical activity stimulates the gut, promoting better digestion and a more diverse microbiome. Additionally, make sure to get enough sleep, as it plays a vital role in gut health and overall well-being.

Conclusion:

In conclusion, maintaining a healthy gut microbiome is of utmost importance for children with Autism Spectrum Disorder and Attention-Deficit/Hyperactivity Disorder. By taking care of your gut, you can positively impact your brain function, reduce inflammation, and improve symptoms associated with these conditions. Make healthy food choices, exercise regularly, and prioritize sleep to support a healthy gut-brain connection. Remember, a healthy gut means a healthy brain and a brighter future!

Gut Microbiome and Autism Spectrum Disorder

The gut-brain connection has become an exciting area of research in recent years, especially when it comes to understanding conditions like Autism Spectrum Disorder (ASD) and Attention Deficit Hyperactivity Disorder (ADHD). In this subchapter, we will explore the fascinating relationship between the gut microbiome and ASD, shedding light on how the two are interconnected.

Did you know that your gut is home to trillions of microorganisms, including bacteria, viruses, and fungi? This community of microorganisms, known as the gut microbiome, plays a vital role in maintaining our overall health. Recent studies have shown that the gut microbiome can influence brain development and function, which has significant implications for children with ASD.

Children with ASD often experience gastrointestinal (GI) issues, such as constipation, diarrhea, and abdominal pain. This has led researchers to investigate whether there is a link between the gut microbiome and the behavioral symptoms associated with ASD. And indeed, they have found some intriguing connections.

Studies have shown that children with ASD tend to have an imbalance in their gut microbiome, with a lower diversity of beneficial bacteria and an overgrowth of harmful bacteria. This dysbiosis can affect the production of certain neurotransmitters, such as serotonin and dopamine, which play a crucial role in regulating mood, behavior, and cognition.

Furthermore, the gut microbiome is involved in the production of short-chain fatty acids (SCFAs), which are essential for maintaining a healthy gut lining and regulating inflammation. Research has found that children with ASD have lower levels of SCFAs, which may contribute to the GI symptoms and behavioral challenges they experience.

Understanding the gut-brain connection in children with ASD opens up new possibilities for treatment and intervention. By focusing on improving the gut microbiome through dietary changes, probiotics, and other interventions, it may be possible to alleviate some of the symptoms associated with ASD.

However, it is important to note that the gut-brain connection is complex, and more research is needed to fully understand how it impacts children with ASD. Each child is unique, and what works for one may not work for another. Therefore, it is always best to consult with healthcare professionals who specialize in gut-brain health when considering interventions.

In conclusion, the gut microbiome plays a significant role in the development and behavior of children with Autism Spectrum Disorder. Exploring the gut-brain connection offers hope for improving their overall well-being and reducing the challenges they face. By understanding and addressing the gut microbiome, we can unlock new possibilities for supporting children with ASD on their journey towards a brighter future.

Altered Gut Microbiome in Children with Autism Spectrum Disorder

The gut-brain connection has been gaining significant attention in recent years, particularly in its role in children with Autism Spectrum Disorder (ASD). ASD is a neurodevelopmental disorder characterized by impaired social interaction, communication difficulties, and repetitive behaviors. In addition to these core symptoms, many children with ASD also experience gastrointestinal problems, such as constipation, diarrhea, and abdominal pain. Researchers have now discovered a link between these gut issues and the altered gut microbiome found in children with ASD.

The gut microbiome refers to the trillions of microorganisms that reside in our digestive tract. These microbes play a crucial role in various bodily functions, including digestion, immune function, and even brain development. Recent studies have found that children with ASD have a distinct composition of gut bacteria compared to their neurotypical peers. This dysbiosis, or imbalance, in the gut microbiome may contribute to the development and severity of ASD symptoms.

So, how does the gut microbiome affect the brain? The gut microbiota produce various metabolites, such as neurotransmitters and short-chain fatty acids, which can directly influence brain function. These metabolites can cross the blood-brain barrier and interact with the central nervous system, affecting behavior, mood, and cognition. Therefore, an altered gut microbiome can potentially disrupt this delicate balance and contribute to the behavioral and cognitive challenges seen in children with ASD.

Understanding the gut-brain connection in children with ASD has significant implications for their treatment and overall well-being. Researchers are exploring the use of probiotics and prebiotics to restore a healthy balance of gut bacteria in children with ASD. By targeting the gut microbiome, it may be possible to alleviate some of the gastrointestinal symptoms and improve cognitive function and behavior.

It's important to note that while the gut-brain connection is particularly relevant for children with ASD, it also extends to children with Attention Deficit Hyperactivity Disorder (ADHD). ADHD is a neurodevelopmental disorder characterized by inattention, hyperactivity, and impulsivity. Similar to ASD, children with ADHD may also experience gastrointestinal issues, suggesting a potential link between their gut microbiome and cognitive function.

In conclusion, the altered gut microbiome found in children with ASD and ADHD highlights the importance of the gut-brain connection in these neurodevelopmental disorders. By understanding and targeting the gut microbiome, researchers and healthcare professionals can potentially improve the symptoms and overall well-being of children with ASD and ADHD. Further research in this area holds promise for developing innovative and personalized interventions that harness the power of the gut-brain connection for these children.

Impact of Gut Microbiome on Autism Spectrum Disorder Symptoms

The gut-brain connection is a fascinating area of research that is shedding light on the complex relationship between our digestive system and our brain. In recent years, scientists have discovered that the gut microbiome, the community of bacteria and other microorganisms that reside in our intestines, plays a crucial role in our overall health and well-being. This is particularly relevant for children with Autism Spectrum Disorder (ASD) and Attention Deficit Hyperactivity Disorder (ADHD).

Research has shown that children with ASD and ADHD often have imbalances in their gut microbiome. These imbalances can lead to a variety of gastrointestinal symptoms, such as constipation, diarrhea, and abdominal pain. More importantly, they can also have a significant impact on the core symptoms of these neurodevelopmental disorders.

One of the key ways in which the gut microbiome affects ASD and ADHD symptoms is through its influence on the immune system. The gut microbiome helps regulate the immune system, and disruptions in its balance can lead to increased inflammation and immune dysregulation. This inflammation can then affect the brain, leading to changes in behavior, mood, and cognitive functioning.

Furthermore, the gut microbiome is also involved in the production of certain neurotransmitters, such as serotonin and dopamine, which play a crucial role in regulating mood and behavior. Imbalances in these neurotransmitters have been linked to the symptoms of ASD and ADHD, including anxiety, impulsivity, and social difficulties.

Fortunately, there are interventions that can help restore balance to the gut microbiome and alleviate some of the symptoms of ASD and ADHD. Probiotics, which are live bacteria and yeasts that can be consumed as supplements or through certain foods, have shown promise in improving gastrointestinal symptoms and reducing behavioral problems in children with ASD and ADHD.

In addition to probiotics, dietary changes can also have a significant impact on the gut microbiome. A diet rich in fiber, whole grains, fruits, and vegetables can help promote the growth of beneficial bacteria in the gut, while reducing the consumption of processed foods and sugar can help starve harmful bacteria.

It is important to note that every child is unique, and what works for one may not work for another. Consulting with a healthcare professional specializing in gut-brain health is essential to develop an individualized treatment plan.

In conclusion, the gut microbiome plays a crucial role in the symptoms of Autism Spectrum Disorder and Attention Deficit Hyperactivity Disorder. By understanding and addressing the imbalances in the gut microbiome, we can potentially improve the overall well-being and quality of life for children with ASD and ADHD.

Gut Microbiome and Attention Deficit Hyperactivity Disorder

Attention Deficit Hyperactivity Disorder (ADHD) is a neurodevelopmental disorder that affects many children worldwide. It is characterized by symptoms such as hyperactivity, impulsivity, and difficulties in sustaining attention. While the precise causes of ADHD remain unclear, recent research has shed light on a potential link between the gut microbiome and this disorder.

The gut microbiome refers to the trillions of microorganisms residing in our digestive system. These microorganisms play a vital role in maintaining our overall health and well-being. Emerging studies suggest that disruptions in the gut microbiome can have negative effects on brain function and behavior, potentially contributing to the development of ADHD.

Research has shown that children with ADHD often have an altered composition of gut bacteria compared to their neurotypical peers. Certain strains of bacteria, such as Bifidobacterium and Lactobacillus, have been found to be decreased in children with ADHD. These bacteria are known to produce neurotransmitters like serotonin and dopamine, which play crucial roles in regulating mood and attention.

Furthermore, studies have revealed a correlation between gut inflammation and ADHD symptoms. Inflammation in the gut can lead to increased permeability of the intestinal lining, allowing harmful substances to enter the bloodstream. This immune response can trigger inflammation in the brain, affecting neurotransmitter function and exacerbating ADHD symptoms.

Understanding the connection between the gut microbiome and ADHD opens up new possibilities for intervention and treatment. Probiotics, which are beneficial bacteria, have shown promise in improving symptoms of ADHD. By restoring a healthy balance of gut bacteria, probiotics may help regulate neurotransmitter production and reduce inflammation.

In addition to probiotics, dietary changes can also have a positive impact on the gut-brain connection in children with ADHD. A diet rich in fiber, fruits, vegetables, and fermented foods can promote the growth of beneficial gut bacteria. On the other hand, processed foods, sugary snacks, and artificial additives can disrupt the gut microbiome and worsen ADHD symptoms.

It is important to note that while the gut microbiome plays a significant role in ADHD, it is not the sole cause of the disorder. ADHD is a complex condition influenced by various genetic, environmental, and neurological factors. However, addressing gut health through the gut-brain connection can potentially provide additional support and improve overall well-being for children with ADHD.

In conclusion, the gut microbiome and its relationship with ADHD is an exciting area of research. Understanding and harnessing the power of the gut-brain connection can offer new insights and strategies for managing ADHD symptoms. By focusing on gut health through probiotics, dietary changes, and other interventions, children with ADHD can potentially experience improvements in attention, behavior, and overall quality of life.

Altered Gut Microbiome in Children with ADHD

One of the fascinating aspects of the gut-brain connection is how it affects children with ADHD. Recent studies have revealed a link between an altered gut microbiome and the symptoms of ADHD in children. The gut microbiome refers to the trillions of microorganisms residing in our digestive system, which play a crucial role in maintaining our overall health.

Children with ADHD often experience challenges with attention, hyperactivity, and impulsivity. These symptoms can significantly impact their daily lives, making it difficult for them to focus in school or engage in social activities. While the exact cause of ADHD is still unknown, researchers have discovered that the gut microbiome may play a significant role in its development and severity.

In children with ADHD, the diversity and abundance of certain gut bacteria differ from those without the condition. Imbalances in the gut microbiome can lead to increased inflammation, impaired neurotransmitter function, and compromised immune responses. These factors can contribute to the symptoms experienced by children with ADHD.

By understanding the link between the gut microbiome and ADHD, we can explore potential interventions to alleviate these symptoms. One promising approach is through dietary changes and probiotic supplementation. Certain foods, such as those rich in fiber and prebiotics, can help nourish the beneficial bacteria in the gut. Probiotics, on the other hand, are live microorganisms that can restore the balance of the gut microbiome.

Research has shown that children with ADHD who received probiotic supplements experienced improvements in their symptoms, including reduced hyperactivity and impulsivity. These findings suggest that modulating the gut microbiome could be a valuable adjunct therapy for children with ADHD.

It is essential to note that the gut-brain connection is complex, and interventions may not work the same for every child with ADHD. However, by exploring the potential of the gut microbiome and its role in ADHD, we can offer children and their families additional tools to manage and alleviate the challenges associated with the condition.

In conclusion, the altered gut microbiome in children with ADHD has emerged as a promising avenue for better understanding and managing the condition. By focusing on the gut-brain connection and exploring interventions such as dietary changes and probiotic supplementation, we can potentially improve the symptoms experienced by children with ADHD. Further research in this area is crucial to develop personalized and effective treatments that harness the power of the gut microbiome for the benefit of children with ADHD.

Connection between Gut Microbiome and ADHD Symptoms

The Connection between Gut Microbiome and ADHD Symptoms

Attention Deficit Hyperactivity Disorder (ADHD) is a neurodevelopmental disorder that affects many children around the world. It is characterized by symptoms such as inattention, hyperactivity, and impulsivity, which can significantly impact a child's daily life. While the exact cause of ADHD is not yet fully understood, recent research has shown a potential link between the gut microbiome and ADHD symptoms.

The gut microbiome refers to the trillions of bacteria and other microorganisms that reside in our digestive system. These tiny organisms play a crucial role in maintaining our overall health, including our brain health. Studies have found that children with ADHD often have an imbalance in their gut microbiome, with lower levels of beneficial bacteria and higher levels of harmful bacteria.

This imbalance in the gut microbiome can have a direct impact on the brain. The gut and the brain are connected through a complex network of nerves called the gut-brain axis. This connection allows signals and molecules to travel between the gut and the brain, influencing various aspects of brain function, including mood, behavior, and cognition.

When the gut microbiome is imbalanced, it can lead to inflammation in the gut, which can then trigger inflammation in the brain. This inflammation can affect neurotransmitter levels, such as dopamine and serotonin, which play a vital role in regulating attention and mood. Imbalances in these neurotransmitters are often observed in individuals with ADHD.

Furthermore, the gut microbiome produces various molecules and metabolites that can affect brain function. For example, certain bacteria in the gut produce short-chain fatty acids, which have been shown to have anti-inflammatory and neuroprotective effects. These molecules can help reduce inflammation in the brain and improve cognitive function.

Addressing the gut microbiome imbalance is becoming an increasingly important aspect of ADHD treatment. Probiotics, which are beneficial bacteria, can be used to restore the balance of the gut microbiome. Studies have shown that certain strains of probiotics, such as Lactobacillus and Bifidobacterium, can improve ADHD symptoms and cognitive function in children.

In addition to probiotics, a healthy diet rich in fiber, fruits, vegetables, and whole grains can also support a healthy gut microbiome. Avoiding processed foods, sugar, and artificial additives is essential to maintain a balanced gut microbiome.

Understanding the connection between the gut microbiome and ADHD symptoms is crucial for children with ADHD and autism. By addressing the gut-brain connection and supporting a healthy gut microbiome, we can potentially improve ADHD symptoms and enhance overall well-being.

Working closely with healthcare professionals, parents, and educators, we can develop holistic approaches to support children with ADHD and autism, taking into account the intricate link between the gut and the brain.

Chapter 3: Gut-Brain Communication Pathways

Overview of Gut-Brain Communication

The gut-brain connection is a fascinating and intricate system that plays a crucial role in the overall health and well-being of children with Autism Spectrum Disorder (ASD) and Attention Deficit Hyperactivity Disorder (ADHD). This subchapter delves into the importance of understanding this connection and how it can positively impact the lives of children with these conditions.

The gut and the brain are connected through a complex network of nerves, chemicals, and hormones. This communication pathway allows the gut to send signals to the brain and vice versa, influencing various aspects of a child's physical and mental health.

For children with ASD, research has shown that they often experience gastrointestinal (GI) issues such as constipation, diarrhea, and abdominal pain. These GI problems can disrupt the balance of good and bad bacteria in the gut, leading to inflammation and an impaired gut-brain communication. By addressing and managing these GI issues, we can potentially improve the symptoms of ASD, including social interaction difficulties, repetitive behaviors, and sensory sensitivities.

Similarly, children with ADHD may also experience gut-related problems. Studies have found a higher prevalence of GI symptoms in children with ADHD compared to their neurotypical peers. These GI issues can contribute to increased levels of inflammation, which in turn affect the brain's functioning and exacerbate ADHD symptoms such as impulsivity, hyperactivity, and inattention.

Understanding and optimizing the gut-brain connection is vital for children with ASD and ADHD. By supporting a healthy gut, we can positively impact brain function, cognition, mood, and behavior. This can be achieved through various interventions, including dietary changes, probiotic supplementation, and addressing food sensitivities.

In this subchapter, we will explore the different strategies and approaches that can help children with ASD and ADHD improve their gut health and strengthen the gut-brain connection. We will discuss the importance of a balanced and nutritious diet, the role of probiotics in promoting a healthy gut microbiome, and the identification and management of food sensitivities.

By taking a holistic approach to the gut-brain connection, we can empower children with ASD and ADHD to thrive both physically and mentally. Through this knowledge, parents, caregivers, and healthcare professionals can work together to provide the best possible support and interventions for these children, helping them reach their full potential.

Bidirectional Communication between the Gut and the Brain

The gut and the brain are two incredibly important organs in our bodies, and they are constantly communicating with each other. This bidirectional communication plays a crucial role in the health and well-being of children with Autism Spectrum Disorder (ASD) and Attention Deficit Hyperactivity Disorder (ADHD). In this subchapter, we will explore the fascinating connection between the gut and the brain and how it can help kids with autism and ADHD.

The gut-brain connection refers to the constant communication and feedback loop between the gut and the brain. This communication occurs through a complex network of nerves, hormones, and chemicals. Recent research has shown that the gut and the brain are intimately connected, and disturbances in this communication can contribute to the symptoms of autism and ADHD.

For children with ASD, studies have found that they often have imbalances in their gut bacteria, known as the gut microbiome. This imbalance can lead to inflammation in the gut, which can then affect the brain. In fact, some researchers believe that the gut microbiome may play a role in the development of ASD. By understanding and addressing these imbalances, we can potentially improve the symptoms of autism in children.

Similarly, children with ADHD may also have imbalances in their gut bacteria. These imbalances can lead to increased inflammation in the gut, which can then affect the brain and contribute to the symptoms of ADHD. By focusing on improving the gut health of children with ADHD, we may be able to reduce their symptoms and improve their overall well-being.

There are several ways to support the gut-brain connection in children with autism and ADHD. One of the most important is through a healthy diet. Consuming a diet rich in fruits, vegetables, whole grains, and lean proteins can help support a healthy gut microbiome. Additionally, avoiding processed foods, artificial additives, and excessive sugar can also be beneficial.

Supplements such as probiotics and omega-3 fatty acids have also shown promise in supporting the gut-brain connection. Probiotics can help restore the balance of good bacteria in the gut, while omega-3 fatty acids have anti-inflammatory properties that can reduce gut inflammation.

In conclusion, the bidirectional communication between the gut and the brain is a crucial aspect of the health and well-being of children with autism and ADHD. By understanding and addressing this connection, we can potentially improve their symptoms and enhance their overall quality of life.

Neurotransmitters and Hormones Involved in Gut-Brain Communication

In this chapter, we will explore the fascinating world of neurotransmitters and hormones that play a crucial role in the communication between our gut and brain. Understanding how these chemicals work is essential for children with ADHD and Autism Spectrum Disorder, as it can help shed light on the connection between their gut health and cognitive function.

Neurotransmitters are chemical messengers that transmit signals between nerve cells in our brain. One important neurotransmitter involved in gut-brain communication is serotonin. Serotonin helps regulate mood, appetite, and sleep, and it also plays a significant role in gastrointestinal function. Research has shown that children with Autism Spectrum Disorder and ADHD often have imbalances in serotonin levels, which can contribute to their symptoms.

Another neurotransmitter of interest is dopamine. Dopamine is associated with pleasure, reward, and motivation. It helps regulate movement, attention, and emotional responses. Studies have found that children with ADHD may have lower levels of dopamine, which can lead to difficulties in focusing and staying motivated.

In addition to neurotransmitters, hormones also play a vital role in the gut-brain connection. One such hormone is oxytocin, often referred to as the "love hormone." Oxytocin is known for its role in bonding, trust, and social interactions. It has been found to have a positive impact on reducing anxiety and improving social behavior in individuals with Autism Spectrum Disorder.

Furthermore, the gut produces a hormone called ghrelin, which regulates hunger and appetite. Ghrelin also has an influence on mood and cognitive function. Imbalances in ghrelin levels can contribute to difficulties in regulating appetite and may affect the overall well-being of children with ADHD and Autism Spectrum Disorder.

Understanding the role of neurotransmitters and hormones in gut-brain communication can help children with ADHD and Autism Spectrum Disorder. By focusing on improving gut health, such as through a healthy diet and targeted supplementation, it is possible to positively impact cognitive function and overall well-being.

In conclusion, the intricate connection between the gut and brain involves a complex interplay of neurotransmitters and hormones. By addressing imbalances in these chemicals, we can potentially improve symptoms associated with ADHD and Autism Spectrum Disorder. It is essential for children and their caregivers to recognize the significance of a healthy gut-brain connection and explore strategies to support its optimal functioning.

Gut-Brain Connection in Autism Spectrum Disorder

As children with ADHD Autism, you may have noticed that your body and mind often feel connected in mysterious ways. And guess what? There's a scientific explanation for it – the Gut-Brain Connection. In this subchapter, we will explore how this connection plays a vital role in Autism Spectrum Disorder (ASD) and how it can help kids with ADHD as well.

The Gut-Brain Connection refers to the constant communication between your gut and your brain. It may sound strange, but did you know that your gut, also known as the "second brain," has millions of nerve cells? These cells send signals to your brain, influencing your emotions, behavior, and even your ability to learn.

For kids with Autism Spectrum Disorder, the Gut-Brain Connection is even more crucial. Researchers have discovered that children with ASD often have imbalances in the bacteria living in their gut. These imbalances can lead to inflammation, affecting the way their brain functions. This is why some kids with ASD experience digestive issues such as constipation, diarrhea, or bloating.

But don't worry – understanding the Gut-Brain Connection can actually be the key to improving your symptoms and overall well-being. By taking care of your gut health, you can support a healthier brain. How? Well, it starts with a healthy diet. Eating foods rich in fiber, like fruits, vegetables, and whole grains, can help promote a diverse and balanced gut microbiome.

Probiotics, which are "good" bacteria, can also be beneficial. They can be found in foods like yogurt, kefir, and sauerkraut. These friendly bacteria help maintain a healthy gut environment and can positively affect your brain function.

In addition to diet, lifestyle factors also play a role in the Gut-Brain Connection. Getting enough sleep, managing stress levels, and engaging in physical activity are all important for maintaining a healthy gut and brain. So, make sure to get enough rest, find healthy ways to cope with stress, and have fun playing outside!

Remember, the Gut-Brain Connection is not just limited to Autism Spectrum Disorder. Kids with ADHD can also benefit from nurturing their gut health. By understanding and taking care of this connection, you are empowering yourself to lead a happier and healthier life.

In conclusion, the Gut-Brain Connection is a fascinating scientific concept that explains the link between your gut and your brain. For children with Autism Spectrum Disorder and ADHD, taking care of their gut health can lead to improvements in their symptoms and overall well-being. By adopting a healthy diet, incorporating probiotics, and practicing healthy lifestyle habits, kids can support a balanced gut microbiome and enhance their brain function. So, embrace the power of the Gut-Brain Connection and unlock your full potential!

Dysregulation of Gut-Brain Communication in Autism Spectrum Disorder

The gut-brain connection is a fascinating and vital aspect of our overall health and well-being. In recent years, researchers have discovered that this connection plays a significant role in the development and management of Autism Spectrum Disorder (ASD). This subchapter aims to shed light on the dysregulation of gut-brain communication in individuals with ASD, specifically addressing children with ADHD and Autism.

Children with Autism Spectrum Disorder often experience various gastrointestinal issues, such as constipation, diarrhea, and abdominal pain. These gut problems can be attributed to the dysregulation of gut-brain communication. The gut and the brain are in constant communication through the vagus nerve, which connects the two and allows for the exchange of information. However, in children with ASD, this communication becomes disrupted, leading to gastrointestinal distress and other related symptoms.

Research has shown that individuals with ASD have an altered gut microbiome, the collection of microorganisms residing in the digestive system. This imbalance in gut bacteria can affect the production of neurotransmitters, the chemicals responsible for transmitting signals in the brain. As a result, children with ASD may experience difficulties in social interaction, communication, and sensory processing.

Understanding the dysregulation of gut-brain communication in ASD is crucial for developing effective interventions and treatments. By focusing on restoring the balance of gut bacteria, we can potentially alleviate some of the symptoms associated with Autism Spectrum Disorder. For example, certain dietary changes, such as incorporating probiotics and prebiotics, have shown promising results in improving gut health and positively impacting behavior and cognition in children with ASD.

Additionally, therapies that target the gut-brain axis, such as gut-directed behavioral therapy and functional medicine approaches, have been successful in managing gastrointestinal symptoms and improving overall well-being in children with ASD. These interventions aim to restore proper communication between the gut and the brain, reducing inflammation and promoting a healthier gut microbiome.

As we continue to unravel the complexities of the gut-brain connection, it becomes evident that addressing gut health is essential for children with Autism Spectrum Disorder and ADHD. By recognizing and targeting the dysregulation of gut-brain communication, we can provide these children with a better quality of life, improved cognitive function, and enhanced social interactions. The journey towards understanding and harnessing the power of the gut-brain connection is ongoing, and it holds great promise for children with these neurodevelopmental disorders.

Implications for Autism Spectrum Disorder Symptoms

Understanding the implications of the gut-brain connection for children with Autism Spectrum Disorder (ASD) is crucial in providing better support and interventions for these young individuals. ASD is a neurodevelopmental disorder characterized by challenges in social interaction, communication difficulties, and repetitive behaviors. However, recent research has shed light on the link between the gut and the brain, offering new insights into the potential management of ASD symptoms.

Children with ASD often experience gastrointestinal (GI) issues such as constipation, diarrhea, and abdominal pain. These symptoms may be related to an imbalance in the gut microbiome, the complex community of microorganisms residing in our intestines. Studies have indicated that individuals with ASD have a different composition of gut bacteria compared to their neurotypical peers. The presence of certain bacteria, or the lack thereof, may contribute to the severity of ASD symptoms.

Moreover, the gut-brain connection plays a vital role in regulating the immune system. Research suggests that children with ASD have an overactive immune response, leading to chronic inflammation in the brain. This inflammation can further impair brain function and exacerbate ASD symptoms. By addressing the gut health of children with ASD, it may be possible to alleviate some of these symptoms and improve overall well-being.

Dietary interventions have shown promise in managing ASD symptoms. Certain foods, such as gluten and casein, have been found to worsen GI symptoms and behavioral issues in children with ASD. Eliminating or reducing the consumption of these substances, as well as implementing a balanced and nutritious diet, can have a positive impact on both gut health and behavior.

Probiotics, the beneficial bacteria found in certain foods and supplements, have also been explored as a potential intervention for ASD. These probiotics can help restore the balance of gut bacteria and reduce inflammation, leading to improvements in behavior and cognitive function.

It is important for parents, caregivers, and healthcare professionals to recognize the implications of the gut-brain connection in children with ASD. By addressing GI issues, reducing inflammation, and implementing dietary interventions, it is possible to enhance the overall well-being and quality of life for children with ASD.

In conclusion, the gut-brain connection has significant implications for children with Autism Spectrum Disorder. By understanding and utilizing this connection, we can potentially alleviate some of the symptoms associated with ASD. Through dietary interventions and probiotic supplementation, we can support a healthy gut microbiome and reduce inflammation, leading to improvements in behavior, cognition, and overall well-being for children with ASD.

Gut-Brain Connection in Attention Deficit Hyperactivity Disorder

Attention Deficit Hyperactivity Disorder (ADHD) is a neurodevelopmental disorder that affects many children around the world. It is characterized by symptoms such as difficulty paying attention, hyperactivity, and impulsivity. While the exact cause of ADHD is still unknown, researchers have discovered a fascinating link between the gut and the brain, known as the gut-brain connection, which may play a role in the development and management of ADHD.

The gut-brain connection refers to the constant communication and interaction between our gut, which houses trillions of bacteria, and our brain. These bacteria, collectively known as the gut microbiota, play a crucial role in maintaining our overall health and well-being. Recent studies have found that imbalances in the gut microbiota may contribute to the symptoms of ADHD.

Children with ADHD often experience digestive issues such as constipation, bloating, and food sensitivities. These symptoms may be linked to an imbalance in the gut bacteria, which can affect the production of neurotransmitters in the brain. Neurotransmitters are chemicals that help regulate our mood, behavior, and attention. When the gut bacteria are not in harmony, it can disrupt the production of these neurotransmitters, leading to symptoms of ADHD.

Furthermore, the gut microbiota also play a role in the body's immune system. Imbalances in the gut bacteria can lead to inflammation, which has been linked to various mental health conditions, including ADHD. Inflammation in the brain can affect its functioning and contribute to the symptoms of ADHD.

Understanding the gut-brain connection is crucial for children with ADHD because it opens up new possibilities for treatment and management. By focusing on improving gut health, we can potentially alleviate some of the symptoms associated with ADHD. This can be achieved through dietary changes, such as incorporating probiotic-rich foods like yogurt and fermented vegetables, and reducing the consumption of processed foods and sugar.

Additionally, certain supplements, such as omega-3 fatty acids and prebiotics, have shown promising results in improving ADHD symptoms by promoting a healthy gut environment. These interventions can help restore the balance of gut bacteria and support optimal brain function.

In conclusion, the gut-brain connection plays a significant role in Attention Deficit Hyperactivity Disorder. By understanding the link between gut health and ADHD symptoms, we can explore new avenues for treatment and management. By prioritizing a healthy gut through diet and supplementation, children with ADHD can potentially experience improvements in their attention, behavior, and overall well-being.

Dysregulation of Gut-Brain Communication in ADHD

Attention Deficit Hyperactivity Disorder (ADHD) is a neurodevelopmental disorder that affects many children worldwide. It is characterized by difficulties in paying attention, hyperactivity, and impulsivity. While the exact cause of ADHD is still unknown, recent research has shown a strong connection between ADHD and the gut-brain communication system.

The gut-brain connection refers to the bidirectional communication between the brain and the gut. This communication occurs through a complex network of nerves, hormones, and neurotransmitters. The gut, also known as the second brain, plays a crucial role in regulating various bodily functions, including mood, behavior, and cognition.

In children with ADHD, this gut-brain communication system is often dysregulated. Research has found that children with ADHD have an imbalance of gut bacteria, known as dysbiosis. This dysbiosis can lead to the production of certain metabolites that can interfere with neurotransmitter function in the brain, contributing to the symptoms of ADHD.

Furthermore, studies have shown that children with ADHD often have increased intestinal permeability, also known as leaky gut. This means that the lining of their intestines is more porous, allowing toxins and undigested food particles to pass through and enter the bloodstream. These substances can trigger an immune response, leading to inflammation in the brain and worsening ADHD symptoms.

The dysregulation of gut-brain communication in ADHD can also affect the production of neurotransmitters such as dopamine and serotonin, which play a crucial role in regulating mood and behavior. Imbalances in these neurotransmitters can contribute to the difficulties in attention and impulse control seen in children with ADHD.

Understanding the dysregulation of gut-brain communication in ADHD opens up new possibilities for treatment and management. By addressing the gut health of children with ADHD, it may be possible to improve their symptoms and overall well-being. This can be achieved through dietary interventions, such as a balanced and nutrient-rich diet, avoiding trigger foods, and incorporating gut-friendly foods such as probiotics and prebiotics.

In conclusion, the dysregulation of gut-brain communication in ADHD plays a significant role in the development and severity of symptoms. By focusing on improving gut health, it is possible to positively impact the symptoms of ADHD and enhance the overall quality of life for children with this disorder.

Impact on ADHD Symptoms and Behavior

Understanding the Gut-Brain Connection for Kids with Autism Spectrum Disorder and ADHD

For children with ADHD and autism, understanding the gut-brain connection is crucial in managing their symptoms and behaviors. Research has shown that there is a strong link between the gut and the brain, and any disruptions in the gut can have a significant impact on a child's overall well-being.

The gut is home to trillions of bacteria, known as the gut microbiota, which play a crucial role in various bodily functions, including digestion, immune system regulation, and even brain development. In recent years, scientists have discovered that the gut microbiota also influences brain function and behavior, making it a potential target for intervention in children with ADHD and autism.

One of the ways the gut-brain connection affects children with ADHD is through inflammation. When the gut is inflamed, it releases certain chemicals that can cross the blood-brain barrier and trigger inflammation in the brain. This inflammation can lead to increased hyperactivity, impulsivity, and difficulty with focus and attention, all hallmark symptoms of ADHD.

Furthermore, imbalances in the gut microbiota can also affect neurotransmitter production and regulation. Neurotransmitters are chemical messengers that help transmit signals in the brain. In children with ADHD, imbalances in neurotransmitters such as dopamine and serotonin have been observed, leading to difficulties in regulating mood, attention, and behavior. By improving the health of the gut microbiota, it is possible to positively influence the production and regulation of these neurotransmitters, potentially reducing ADHD symptoms.

Additionally, the gut-brain connection can impact behavior in children with autism. Many children with autism also experience gastrointestinal issues such as constipation, diarrhea, or abdominal pain. These gastrointestinal problems can exacerbate their autistic symptoms, leading to increased irritability, aggression, and difficulty with social interactions. By addressing and improving gut health, it is possible to alleviate these symptoms and improve overall behavior in children with autism.

In conclusion, the gut-brain connection plays a significant role in the symptoms and behaviors exhibited by children with ADHD and autism. By understanding and addressing this connection, parents, caregivers, and healthcare professionals can develop effective strategies to manage and improve the well-being of these children. From reducing inflammation to balancing neurotransmitters and alleviating gastrointestinal issues, the gut-brain connection offers hope for a brighter future for children with ADHD and autism.

Chapter 4: Strategies for Supporting the Gut-Brain Connection

Dietary Interventions for Autism Spectrum Disorder

When it comes to managing Autism Spectrum Disorder (ASD), dietary interventions have emerged as a promising avenue for improving symptoms and enhancing overall well-being. Research has shown that there is a strong connection between the gut and the brain, and understanding this link can be particularly beneficial for children with ASD and ADHD.

The gut-brain connection refers to the intricate relationship between the digestive system and the brain. It is believed that imbalances in the gut can contribute to neurological and behavioral issues, including those associated with ASD and ADHD. By addressing these imbalances through dietary interventions, we can potentially alleviate some of the challenges faced by children with these conditions.

One of the key dietary interventions for ASD is the implementation of a gluten-free and casein-free (GFCF) diet. Gluten is a protein found in wheat and other grains, while casein is a protein found in milk and dairy products. Some individuals with ASD may have sensitivities or intolerances to these proteins, which can trigger inflammation and affect brain function. By eliminating gluten and casein from their diet, children with ASD may experience a reduction in symptoms such as social withdrawal, repetitive behaviors, and communication difficulties.

Additionally, incorporating nutrient-dense foods that support gut health can also be beneficial for children with ASD and ADHD. Probiotics, for example, are beneficial bacteria that can help restore a healthy balance in the gut microbiome. These live microorganisms can be found in certain foods like yogurt, sauerkraut, and kimchi, or can be taken as supplements. By promoting a healthy gut environment, probiotics may help improve cognitive function, behavior, and overall well-being.

Furthermore, certain vitamins and minerals have been shown to play a crucial role in brain health and function. For instance, omega-3 fatty acids found in fatty fish like salmon and mackerel, as well as in flaxseeds and walnuts, are essential for brain development and cognitive function. Studies have indicated that supplementation with omega-3 fatty acids may reduce hyperactivity and impulsivity in children with ADHD.

It is important to note that dietary interventions should be implemented under the guidance of healthcare professionals. Each child is unique, and what works for one may not work for another. Keeping a food journal and monitoring any changes in symptoms can help identify specific triggers and tailor the dietary interventions accordingly.

In conclusion, the gut-brain connection offers valuable insights into managing ASD and ADHD symptoms. By implementing dietary interventions such as a GFCF diet, incorporating probiotics, and ensuring adequate intake of essential nutrients, we can potentially improve the overall well-being and quality of life for children with these conditions. It is an exciting field of research that continues to provide hope and new possibilities for children with ASD and ADHD.

Gluten-Free and Casein-Free Diet

For children with ADHD and autism, maintaining a healthy diet is crucial to promoting optimal brain function and overall well-being. One popular dietary approach that has shown promising results is the gluten-free and casein-free (GFCF) diet. This subchapter delves into the benefits and implementation of this diet, providing essential information for parents and caregivers.

The gut-brain connection plays a significant role in children with autism spectrum disorder (ASD) and ADHD. Research has shown that certain food components, such as gluten (a protein found in wheat and other grains) and casein (a protein found in milk and dairy products), can negatively affect the gut and subsequently impact neurological functioning. By eliminating these substances from the diet, many children have experienced improvements in behavior, cognition, and overall functioning.

When following a GFCF diet, it is essential to carefully read food labels and avoid any products containing gluten or casein. This may involve substituting gluten-containing grains like wheat, barley, and rye with gluten-free alternatives such as rice, quinoa, and corn. Similarly, dairy products like milk, cheese, and yogurt should be replaced with non-dairy alternatives such as almond milk, coconut milk, or soy-based products.

It is worth noting that implementing a GFCF diet requires dedication and perseverance. Parents and caregivers should work closely with healthcare professionals and nutritionists to ensure that the child receives all necessary nutrients. Vitamin and mineral supplements may be recommended to compensate for any potential deficiencies.

While the GFCF diet has shown positive results for many children with ADHD and autism, it is important to understand that each child is unique. Some may respond better to this dietary approach than others. It is crucial to monitor the child's progress and consult with healthcare professionals to assess the effectiveness and make any necessary adjustments.

In conclusion, the gluten-free and casein-free diet can be a valuable tool in managing ADHD and autism symptoms. By eliminating gluten and casein from the diet, children may experience improved gut health, leading to better cognitive function and behavior. However, it is essential to work closely with healthcare professionals and nutritionists to ensure the child's nutritional needs are met.

Probiotics and Prebiotics for Gut Health

The gut-brain connection is a fascinating field of study that explores the relationship between our gut health and our mental well-being. It is especially important for children with Autism Spectrum Disorder (ASD) and Attention Deficit Hyperactivity Disorder (ADHD) to understand the impact of this connection on their overall health.

One key aspect of maintaining a healthy gut is through the use of probiotics and prebiotics. Probiotics are live bacteria that are beneficial to our digestive system and can help restore the balance of good bacteria in our gut. Prebiotics, on the other hand, are a type of fiber that acts as food for the probiotics, allowing them to thrive and provide their health benefits.

For children with ASD, studies have shown that there is often an imbalance in the gut bacteria, known as dysbiosis. This imbalance can lead to increased inflammation in the body and potentially contribute to the symptoms associated with ASD, such as digestive issues, anxiety, and behavioral challenges. By introducing probiotics into their diet, we can help restore this balance and potentially alleviate some of these symptoms.

Similarly, children with ADHD may also benefit from incorporating probiotics and prebiotics into their daily routine. Research has indicated that individuals with ADHD often have altered gut microbiota, which can affect their cognitive function and behavior. By promoting a healthy gut environment, we may be able to support better attention and focus, as well as improved mood regulation.

When selecting probiotics and prebiotics for your child, it is important to consult with a healthcare professional or a registered dietitian who specializes in gut health. They can help you choose the most appropriate strains of probiotics and the right types of prebiotic fibers for your child's specific needs.

Incorporating probiotics and prebiotics into your child's diet can be done through various sources such as yogurt, kefir, sauerkraut, kimchi, and certain types of fermented foods. Additionally, there are also probiotic and prebiotic supplements available, which can be a convenient option for ensuring your child is getting the necessary beneficial bacteria and fiber.

Remember, every child is unique, and what works for one may not work for another. It is essential to monitor your child's response to probiotics and prebiotics and make adjustments as necessary. With proper guidance and support, optimizing gut health through probiotics and prebiotics may contribute to a healthier gut-brain connection and improved overall well-being for children with ASD and ADHD.

Dietary Interventions for Attention Deficit Hyperactivity Disorder

In recent years, there has been a growing interest in understanding the connection between the gut and the brain when it comes to managing neurodevelopmental disorders such as Autism Spectrum Disorder (ASD) and Attention Deficit Hyperactivity Disorder (ADHD). This subchapter will explore the dietary interventions that can be implemented to help children with ADHD and Autism.

Research has shown that certain foods and nutrients can influence brain function and behavior. By making strategic dietary changes, we can potentially alleviate some of the symptoms associated with ADHD and Autism. It is important to note that dietary interventions should always be done under the guidance of a healthcare professional or a registered dietitian.

One dietary intervention that has shown promising results is the elimination of certain food additives and allergens. Studies have found that artificial food coloring, preservatives, and flavor enhancers can worsen hyperactivity and impulsivity in children with ADHD. Additionally, some individuals may have sensitivities or allergies to common allergens such as gluten, dairy, or soy.

Identifying and eliminating these trigger foods can lead to a reduction in symptoms.

Another approach is to focus on a nutrient-rich diet. Essential nutrients like omega-3 fatty acids, vitamins, and minerals are crucial for brain health and function. Increasing the consumption of foods rich in these nutrients, such as fatty fish, leafy greens, nuts, and seeds, can potentially improve attention, focus, and cognitive abilities in children with ADHD and Autism.

Probiotics, which are beneficial bacteria that promote a healthy gut microbiome, have also shown promise in managing neurodevelopmental disorders. Studies have found a link between imbalanced gut bacteria and behavioral symptoms in children with ADHD and Autism. By incorporating probiotic-rich foods like yogurt, kefir, and sauerkraut, or taking probiotic supplements, we can potentially restore the balance of gut bacteria and improve symptoms.

It is important to remember that every child is unique, and what works for one may not work for another. It is recommended to keep a food diary to track any changes in behavior or symptoms after implementing dietary interventions. Consulting with a healthcare professional or a registered dietitian can provide personalized guidance and ensure that the child's nutritional needs are met.

In conclusion, dietary interventions can be a valuable tool in managing the symptoms of ADHD and Autism. By eliminating trigger foods, focusing on a nutrient-rich diet, and incorporating probiotics, we can potentially improve brain function and behavior in children with these neurodevelopmental disorders. However, it is essential to work closely with healthcare professionals in order to create an individualized plan that suits the child's specific needs.

Elimination Diets and Food Sensitivities

One of the key factors in understanding the gut-brain connection for kids with Autism Spectrum Disorder (ASD) and Attention Deficit Hyperactivity Disorder (ADHD) is examining the role of elimination diets and food sensitivities. Many children with these conditions often experience gastrointestinal issues, which can exacerbate their symptoms and make it difficult for them to function optimally.

An elimination diet involves removing certain foods from a child's diet to identify potential triggers for their symptoms. This approach aims to pinpoint specific food sensitivities that may be contributing to their gut and brain health issues. By eliminating these trigger foods, parents and caregivers can observe if there is an improvement in the child's behavior, attention, and overall well-being.

Food sensitivities can manifest in various ways, including digestive problems, skin issues, mood swings, and cognitive difficulties. Dairy products, gluten, artificial additives, and certain food colorings are common culprits that can worsen symptoms in children with ASD and ADHD. However, it's important to note that not all children will have the same sensitivities, and what works for one child may not work for another.

When embarking on an elimination diet, it is crucial to work with healthcare professionals, such as pediatricians, dietitians, or nutritionists, who specialize in these conditions. They can guide parents in creating a well-balanced and nutritious meal plan that avoids trigger foods while ensuring the child receives all the necessary nutrients for their growth and development.

Elimination diets should be implemented for a specific duration, typically a few weeks, to allow sufficient time for the body to eliminate any potential allergens. After this period, certain foods can be gradually reintroduced, one at a time, to determine if they elicit any adverse reactions. This process helps identify the specific trigger foods, enabling parents to develop a long-term dietary plan that supports their child's gut and brain health.

It is essential to approach elimination diets and food sensitivities with patience and an open mind. While some children may experience significant improvements in their symptoms, others may not see the same level of benefit. The gut-brain connection is complex, and there are various factors that contribute to its functioning. Nonetheless, identifying and addressing food sensitivities can be a valuable step towards supporting the overall well-being of children with ASD and ADHD.

In conclusion, elimination diets and understanding food sensitivities play a significant role in the gut-brain connection for kids with Autism Spectrum Disorder and Attention Deficit Hyperactivity Disorder. By identifying trigger foods and making appropriate dietary changes, parents can potentially alleviate symptoms and improve their child's quality of life. However, it is vital to consult healthcare professionals and approach these dietary modifications with caution and careful monitoring.

Omega-3 Fatty Acids and Their Role in ADHD

In recent years, there has been growing interest in the role of omega-3 fatty acids in the management of attention deficit hyperactivity disorder (ADHD). Omega-3 fatty acids are a type of polyunsaturated fat that are vital for our overall health, particularly brain health. They are commonly found in fatty fish like salmon, mackerel, and sardines, as well as in walnuts, flaxseeds, and chia seeds.

Research suggests that children with ADHD often have lower levels of omega-3 fatty acids in their bodies compared to their neurotypical peers. Studies have shown that supplementing with omega-3 fatty acids may help improve symptoms of ADHD, such as impulsivity, hyperactivity, and inattention.

One of the main ways in which omega-3 fatty acids benefit children with ADHD is by reducing inflammation in the brain. Inflammation is a natural response by the body to injury or infection, but chronic inflammation can be detrimental to brain function. Omega-3 fatty acids have anti-inflammatory properties that help to calm the brain and improve its overall functioning.

Furthermore, omega-3 fatty acids are crucial for the development and maintenance of healthy brain cells. They play a vital role in the communication between brain cells, which is essential for proper cognitive function. By ensuring an adequate supply of omega-3 fatty acids, we can support optimal brain development and functioning in children with ADHD.

Omega-3 fatty acids have also been shown to have a positive impact on mood and behavior. Many children with ADHD experience mood swings, irritability, and difficulty regulating their emotions. Omega-3 fatty acids can help to stabilize mood and promote a more balanced emotional state.

While omega-3 fatty acids can be obtained through a healthy diet, it may be challenging for children with ADHD and autism to consume enough of these foods consistently. In such cases, supplementation with omega-3 fatty acids may be beneficial. It is important to consult with a healthcare professional before starting any new supplements to determine the appropriate dosage and ensure safety.

In conclusion, omega-3 fatty acids play a significant role in supporting brain health and improving symptoms of ADHD. By incorporating omega-3-rich foods into the diet or considering supplementation, children with ADHD can potentially experience improved attention, reduced hyperactivity, and better overall cognitive function. The gut-brain connection is crucial in understanding how certain nutrients, like omega-3 fatty acids, can positively impact neurodevelopmental disorders such as autism spectrum disorder and ADHD.

Lifestyle Factors and Gut-Brain Connection

In this subchapter, we will explore the fascinating link between lifestyle factors and the gut-brain connection in children with Autism Spectrum

Disorder (ASD) and Attention Deficit Hyperactivity Disorder (ADHD).
Understanding how these lifestyle factors can impact their gut and brain health
is crucial for children with these conditions.

The gut-brain connection refers to the bidirectional communication between
the gastrointestinal system and the brain. It is a complex network of nerves,
hormones, and chemicals that allows the gut and the brain to influence each
other. Research has shown that imbalances in the gut microbiome, the
community of microorganisms living in our intestines, can have a profound
effect on brain function and behavior.

One lifestyle factor that significantly impacts the gut-brain connection is diet.
Children with ASD and ADHD often have specific dietary needs, and certain
foods can exacerbate their symptoms. For example, gluten and casein, found in
wheat and dairy products, respectively, have been shown to increase
inflammation in the gut and disrupt brain function in some individuals. By
adopting a specialized diet, such as a gluten-free and casein-free diet, children
may experience improvements in their behavioral and cognitive functioning.

Another crucial lifestyle factor is sleep. Children with ASD and ADHD often
struggle with sleep problems, which can further disrupt the delicate balance of
the gut-brain connection. Sleep deprivation has been linked to increased
inflammation, altered hormone levels, and impaired cognitive function.
Implementing a consistent sleep routine and creating a conducive sleep
environment can help improve sleep quality and, in turn, support the gut-brain
connection.

Physical activity is also essential for maintaining a healthy gut-brain
connection. Regular exercise has been shown to reduce inflammation, enhance
neurotransmitter production, and improve cognitive function. Engaging in
activities such as swimming, biking, or playing team sports can not only
improve physical health but also support optimal brain function for children
with ASD and ADHD.

Lastly, managing stress is vital for maintaining a healthy gut-brain connection. Stress can disrupt the balance of gut bacteria, leading to gastrointestinal issues and exacerbating symptoms of ASD and ADHD. Encouraging relaxation techniques like deep breathing, mindfulness, and engaging in hobbies or activities that bring joy can help reduce stress levels and support a healthy gut-brain connection.

By understanding and implementing lifestyle factors that support the gut-brain connection, children with ASD and ADHD can experience improvements in their overall well-being. Through a specialized diet, quality sleep, regular exercise, and stress management, we can empower these children to thrive and reach their full potential.

Importance of Physical Activity and Exercise

The Importance of Physical Activity and Exercise for Children with ADHD and Autism

Physical activity and exercise play a crucial role in the overall well-being and development of children with ADHD and Autism Spectrum Disorder (ASD). Not only does regular physical activity benefit their physical health, but it also has a profound impact on their mental and emotional well-being. In this subchapter, we will explore the significance of physical activity and exercise for children with ADHD and Autism, and how it contributes to the gut-brain connection.

Physical activity has been proven to have numerous benefits for children with ADHD and Autism. It helps improve their focus, attention, and self-control, which are often challenging for them. Engaging in physical activities such as running, swimming, or playing sports can help children with ADHD and Autism regulate their energy levels, reduce impulsivity, and improve their ability to concentrate. Moreover, exercise stimulates the release of endorphins, which are natural mood elevators, helping children feel happier and more relaxed.

Regular physical activity is also closely linked to the gut-brain connection for kids with Autism Spectrum Disorder. Research has shown that exercise can positively impact the gut microbiome, which plays a crucial role in the overall health of the brain and body. By promoting a diverse and healthy gut microbiome, physical activity can support better digestion, reduce gut inflammation, and enhance the absorption of essential nutrients. This, in turn, can have a positive effect on cognitive abilities, behavior, and overall brain health.

For children with ADHD, physical activity and exercise are equally essential. While these children often struggle with hyperactivity and restlessness, engaging in regular physical activities can help them channel their energy in a productive and controlled manner. Physical activity can also reduce stress and anxiety, which are common symptoms of ADHD. By promoting relaxation and improved sleep patterns, exercise can contribute to better focus and attention span during daytime activities.

In conclusion, physical activity and exercise are of utmost importance for children with ADHD and Autism. It not only enhances their physical health but also contributes significantly to their mental and emotional well-being. By incorporating regular physical activities into their daily routines, children with ADHD and Autism can experience improved focus, attention, self-control, and overall brain health. Additionally, physical activity supports the gut-brain connection, promoting a healthy gut microbiome and reducing symptoms related to digestion and inflammation. It is crucial for parents, educators, and healthcare professionals to encourage and facilitate regular physical activity and exercise for children with ADHD and Autism Spectrum Disorder, as it can be a powerful tool in their journey towards a healthier and happier life.

Managing Stress for Optimal Gut-Brain Health

Stress is a common experience that affects everyone, including children with ADHD and autism. However, managing stress is crucial for maintaining optimal gut-brain health in these individuals. The gut-brain connection is a complex relationship between the gut (digestive system) and the brain, where they constantly communicate and influence each other. Understanding this connection can help children with autism and ADHD lead healthier and happier lives.

Stress has a direct impact on the gut-brain connection. When we are stressed, our body releases a hormone called cortisol, which can disrupt the balance of bacteria in our gut. This imbalance can lead to a variety of gut-related issues such as bloating, constipation, and diarrhea. Moreover, research has shown that stress can worsen the symptoms of both autism and ADHD, making it even more important to manage stress effectively.

There are several strategies that children with autism and ADHD can use to manage stress and promote optimal gut-brain health. One effective approach is to incorporate relaxation techniques into their daily routine. Deep breathing exercises, meditation, and yoga can all help reduce stress levels and promote a sense of calmness. Additionally, engaging in regular physical activity, such as bike riding or playing a sport, can also help alleviate stress and improve overall well-being.

Another crucial aspect of managing stress is maintaining a healthy diet. Certain foods, such as those high in sugar and processed ingredients, can contribute to gut inflammation and exacerbate stress levels. Encouraging children to consume a balanced diet rich in fruits, vegetables, and whole grains can help support a healthy gut and reduce stress. Additionally, including probiotic-rich foods, such as yogurt and fermented vegetables, can promote a healthy balance of gut bacteria.

Creating a structured environment and establishing a consistent routine can also help children with autism and ADHD manage stress. Predictability and familiarity can reduce anxiety and provide a sense of stability. Ensuring that they have enough sleep is also crucial, as lack of sleep can increase stress levels and negatively impact gut health.

In conclusion, managing stress is vital for promoting optimal gut-brain health in children with ADHD and autism. By incorporating relaxation techniques, maintaining a healthy diet, creating a structured environment, and ensuring enough sleep, children can reduce stress levels and support a healthy gut-brain connection. These strategies can ultimately lead to improved overall well-being and better management of symptoms associated with autism and ADHD.

Chapter 5: Integrative Approaches for Holistic Support

Mind-Body Practices for Autism Spectrum Disorder

In this subchapter, we will explore the incredible benefits of mind-body practices for children with Autism Spectrum Disorder (ASD). These practices can play a crucial role in improving the overall well-being of children with ASD, and can also help manage symptoms related to attention deficit hyperactivity disorder (ADHD).

The gut-brain connection is a fascinating area of study that highlights the intricate relationship between our digestive system and our brain. This connection is particularly significant for children with ASD and ADHD, as they often experience gastrointestinal issues alongside their neurological challenges.

Mind-body practices such as yoga, meditation, and deep breathing exercises have been found to have a positive impact on the gut-brain connection, leading to improved symptoms and overall quality of life for children with ASD and ADHD. These practices help regulate the autonomic nervous system, which plays a vital role in managing stress, anxiety, and emotional regulation.

Yoga, for example, combines gentle movements with deep breathing and mindfulness, promoting relaxation and reducing stress levels in children. Regular yoga practice has been shown to improve sleep patterns, decrease hyperactivity, and enhance focus and attention span.

Meditation, on the other hand, helps children with ASD and ADHD develop self-awareness and mindfulness. By learning to focus their attention and let go of intrusive thoughts, children can experience a greater sense of calm and stability. This practice has been linked to reduced anxiety levels, improved emotional regulation, and enhanced cognitive abilities.

Deep breathing exercises are simple yet powerful tools that can be easily incorporated into daily routines. By taking slow, deep breaths, children activate the parasympathetic nervous system, which is responsible for the body's relaxation response. This, in turn, helps reduce stress and anxiety, leading to improved overall well-being.

Integrating mind-body practices into the daily lives of children with ASD and ADHD can have remarkable effects on their gut-brain connection. These practices provide them with valuable tools to manage stress, regulate emotions, and enhance their overall mental and physical health.

It is essential to consult with healthcare professionals and specialized therapists to determine which mind-body practices are most suitable for each individual child. By incorporating these practices into their daily routines, children with ASD and ADHD can experience significant improvements in their overall well-being and quality of life.

Yoga and Meditation for Stress Reduction

In this subchapter, we will explore the incredible benefits of yoga and meditation for stress reduction in children with ADHD and Autism Spectrum Disorder (ASD). These ancient practices have been found to be highly effective in promoting mental and emotional well-being, and can significantly improve the lives of children with these conditions.

The Gut-Brain Connection for Kids with Autism Spectrum Disorder and ADHD is a complex and fascinating topic. It is well known that individuals with these conditions often experience higher levels of stress and anxiety compared to their neurotypical peers. This can be due to various factors, including sensory sensitivities, difficulty with social interactions, and challenges in managing everyday tasks.

Yoga and meditation offer a holistic approach to managing stress and promoting overall well-being. The physical postures, breathing exercises, and mindfulness techniques involved in yoga help children with ADHD and ASD develop better self-regulation skills. Through regular practice, they learn to focus their attention, calm their minds, and release tension from their bodies.

For children with ADHD, yoga can be particularly beneficial. The practice of yoga helps improve attention and concentration, enhance executive functioning skills, and reduce hyperactivity. The combination of physical movement, deep breathing, and mindfulness creates a sense of calm and stability, allowing children to better manage their symptoms and perform daily tasks more efficiently.

Similarly, children with Autism Spectrum Disorder can greatly benefit from yoga and meditation. The structured nature of yoga classes provides a predictable and safe environment, which is especially important for individuals with ASD who thrive on routine and familiarity. By engaging in yoga, children with ASD can improve body awareness, coordination, and balance, while also reducing anxiety and promoting relaxation.

Meditation, another key aspect of this subchapter, further complements the practice of yoga. Through guided imagery and mindful breathing exercises, children with ADHD and ASD can develop a greater sense of self-awareness and emotional regulation. Meditation helps to quiet the mind, reduce racing thoughts, and cultivate a sense of inner peace.

In conclusion, incorporating yoga and meditation into the lives of children with ADHD and Autism Spectrum Disorder can have profound effects on their overall well-being. By reducing stress, improving self-regulation, and promoting relaxation, these practices empower children to better navigate the challenges they face on a daily basis. The Gut-Brain Connection for Kids with Autism Spectrum Disorder and ADHD can be strengthened through the regular practice of yoga and meditation, leading to a more balanced and fulfilling life.

Sensory Integration Techniques

In this subchapter, we will explore the powerful world of sensory integration techniques and how they can benefit children with ADHD and Autism Spectrum Disorder (ASD). These techniques aim to help children better understand and respond to their surroundings by promoting the integration of sensory information within the brain.

For children with ADHD and ASD, sensory processing can often be challenging. They may struggle with sensory overload or have difficulty interpreting and responding to sensory stimuli. Sensory integration techniques can play a crucial role in helping these children regulate their senses, improve focus, and enhance their overall well-being.

One effective technique is deep pressure therapy, which involves applying firm and gentle pressure to the body. This can be achieved through activities such as weighted blankets, compression clothing, or even hugs. Deep pressure therapy has been shown to have a calming effect on the nervous system, helping children feel more grounded and focused.

Another powerful technique is sensory diet, which involves creating a personalized schedule of sensory activities throughout the day. These activities can include swinging, jumping on a trampoline, or engaging in tactile play with materials like sand or playdough. By incorporating these sensory experiences into their daily routines, children can improve their ability to process and respond to sensory information.

Furthermore, sensory integration techniques often involve providing children with a variety of sensory inputs to help them develop their sensory processing skills. This can be done through activities like therapy balls, balance boards, or textured surfaces. By engaging in these activities, children can strengthen their sensory systems and improve their ability to cope with different sensory stimuli.

It is important to note that each child is unique, and what works for one may not work for another. Therefore, it is essential to work closely with therapists, educators, and parents to determine the most effective sensory integration techniques for each child.

In conclusion, sensory integration techniques can be incredibly beneficial for children with ADHD and Autism Spectrum Disorder. By promoting the integration of sensory information within the brain, these techniques help children regulate their senses, improve focus, and enhance overall well-being. By incorporating techniques such as deep pressure therapy, sensory diets, and providing a variety of sensory inputs, children can develop their sensory processing skills and navigate the world with greater ease.

Mind-Body Practices for Attention Deficit Hyperactivity Disorder

In this subchapter, we will explore the beneficial mind-body practices that can help children with Attention Deficit Hyperactivity Disorder (ADHD) manage their symptoms and improve their overall well-being. These practices, when combined with a better understanding of the gut-brain connection, can greatly enhance the lives of children with ADHD.

One of the most effective mind-body practices for children with ADHD is mindfulness meditation. By learning to focus their attention on the present moment, children with ADHD can improve their ability to concentrate and reduce impulsivity. Mindfulness exercises, such as deep breathing and body scans, can help children develop awareness of their thoughts and feelings, allowing them to better regulate their behavior.

Another valuable practice is yoga. Yoga combines physical postures, breathing techniques, and meditation to promote relaxation and balance in the mind and body. Regular yoga practice can help children with ADHD improve their self-control, increase their attention span, and reduce hyperactivity. Additionally, yoga can improve sleep quality, which is often disrupted in children with ADHD.

Exercise is also crucial for children with ADHD. Engaging in physical activities such as running, swimming, or playing sports releases endorphins, which are natural mood enhancers. Regular exercise not only helps reduce hyperactivity and impulsivity but also improves focus and attention. Encouraging children with ADHD to participate in activities they enjoy can be an effective way to incorporate exercise into their daily routine.

Furthermore, biofeedback is a mind-body technique that can benefit children with ADHD. It involves using electronic devices to monitor and provide feedback on physiological processes such as heart rate, muscle tension, and brainwaves. Through biofeedback, children can learn to recognize the physical signs of their ADHD symptoms and develop strategies to manage them effectively.

By incorporating these mind-body practices into their daily lives, children with ADHD can experience significant improvements in their symptoms and overall well-being. The gut-brain connection plays a vital role in understanding and managing ADHD, and these practices can further strengthen this connection. By combining a healthy gut and a balanced mind, children with ADHD can lead happier, more fulfilling lives.

Mindfulness and Attention Training

In today's fast-paced world, it can be challenging for children with ADHD and autism to stay focused and attentive. However, with the help of mindfulness and attention training, these children can enhance their ability to concentrate, regulate their emotions, and improve their overall well-being.

Mindfulness is the practice of paying attention to the present moment without judgment. By teaching children with ADHD and autism to be aware of their thoughts, feelings, and bodily sensations, mindfulness enables them to engage more effectively with their surroundings. This technique has been proven to reduce stress, anxiety, and impulsivity in children with neurodevelopmental disorders.

Attention training, on the other hand, involves exercises and strategies to improve concentration and focus. It helps children with ADHD and autism to strengthen their attention span and resist distractions. By training their minds to stay on task, these children can better engage in learning and social interactions.

The gut-brain connection plays a crucial role in the effectiveness of mindfulness and attention training for children with autism and ADHD. Recent research has shown that the gut microbiome, the collection of microorganisms residing in our digestive tract, can influence brain function and behavior. Imbalances in the gut microbiome have been linked to neurodevelopmental disorders, including autism and ADHD.

By promoting a healthy gut microbiome through proper nutrition and supplementation, children can optimize their brain health and improve their ability to benefit from mindfulness and attention training. Foods rich in fiber, such as fruits, vegetables, and whole grains, support the growth of beneficial gut bacteria. Probiotics, which are live bacteria and yeasts that are good for our health, can also be helpful in rebalancing the gut microbiome.

In conclusion, mindfulness and attention training are powerful tools for children with ADHD and autism to enhance their cognitive abilities, emotional regulation, and overall well-being. When combined with a focus on nurturing a healthy gut-brain connection through proper nutrition and supplementation, these techniques can have a profound impact on the lives of these children. With mindfulness and attention training, children can unlock their full potential and thrive in a world that often feels overwhelming to them.

Biofeedback and Neurofeedback

In the exploration of the gut-brain connection for kids with Autism Spectrum Disorder (ASD) and Attention Deficit Hyperactivity Disorder (ADHD), two powerful tools have emerged: biofeedback and neurofeedback. These innovative techniques offer promising avenues for managing and improving the symptoms of these conditions.

Biofeedback is a non-invasive approach that focuses on enhancing self-regulation skills. It involves using electronic sensors to monitor and measure physiological responses in the body, such as heart rate, muscle tension, and skin temperature. By observing these signals in real-time, children with ASD and ADHD can learn to recognize and control their bodily functions, leading to improved emotional and cognitive well-being.

For children with ASD, biofeedback can be particularly helpful in addressing sensory processing challenges. By teaching them to self-regulate their physiological responses, it can assist in reducing anxiety, improving attention, and enhancing social interactions. Through biofeedback, children learn to identify triggers that may overwhelm their senses and develop strategies to manage them effectively.

Similarly, neurofeedback taps into the power of the brain to promote self-regulation. This technique involves measuring brainwave activity through an electroencephalogram (EEG) and providing real-time feedback to the individual. By observing their brainwave patterns, children with ASD and ADHD can learn to modify and regulate their brain activity, leading to improved focus, attention, and behavioral control.

Neurofeedback has shown great promise in addressing the core symptoms of ASD and ADHD. By training the brain to produce specific brainwave patterns associated with calmness and attention, children can experience significant improvements in their ability to concentrate and manage impulsive behaviors. Over time, the brain learns to self-regulate, leading to long-lasting benefits.

Both biofeedback and neurofeedback offer safe and drug-free alternatives for managing the symptoms of ASD and ADHD. They empower children to take an active role in their treatment and provide them with valuable skills for self-regulation. By harnessing the power of the gut-brain connection, these techniques hold great potential in improving the lives of children with these conditions.

However, it is important to note that biofeedback and neurofeedback should always be utilized under the guidance of trained professionals. A comprehensive assessment and individualized treatment plan are essential to ensure that these techniques are tailored to the specific needs of each child.

In conclusion, biofeedback and neurofeedback are valuable tools in the exploration of the gut-brain connection for children with Autism Spectrum Disorder and Attention Deficit Hyperactivity Disorder. By promoting self-regulation and enhancing brain function, these techniques offer hope and opportunities for improved outcomes in managing the symptoms of these conditions. With further research and advancements in the field, biofeedback and neurofeedback hold the potential to revolutionize the treatment of ASD and ADHD, providing a brighter future for children with these challenges.

Collaborative Care for Optimal Results

When it comes to addressing the challenges faced by children with Autism Spectrum Disorder (ASD) and Attention Deficit Hyperactivity Disorder (ADHD), collaboration is key. The gut-brain connection plays a crucial role in the development and management of these conditions, and by working together, we can achieve optimal results for our children.

The gut-brain connection refers to the link between the gut and the brain, and how the health of one affects the other. In recent years, there has been a growing body of research highlighting the impact of gut health on neurodevelopmental disorders like ASD and ADHD. This connection offers new possibilities for treatment and management, paving the way for collaborative care.

Collaborative care involves a multidisciplinary approach, where healthcare professionals, educators, therapists, and parents work together to create a comprehensive treatment plan. By combining their expertise, knowledge, and resources, they can address the various aspects of a child's condition and provide the best possible support.

For children with ASD, collaborative care focuses on improving gut health through dietary modifications, supplementation, and probiotics. A team of healthcare professionals, including pediatricians, gastroenterologists, and nutritionists, can work together to design a personalized diet that supports the gut-brain connection. They can provide guidance on the elimination of certain foods that may trigger symptoms and recommend the inclusion of nutrient-dense foods that promote gut health.

Similarly, for children with ADHD, collaborative care can involve a holistic approach that includes medication, behavioral therapy, and dietary interventions. By collaborating with healthcare providers, therapists, and educators, parents can create an environment that supports their child's unique needs. This may involve implementing strategies to improve focus and attention, creating structured routines, and incorporating brain-boosting foods into their diet.

Collaborative care also extends to the educational setting. Teachers and school administrators can work with parents and healthcare professionals to develop individualized education plans (IEPs) that cater to the specific needs of children with ASD or ADHD. By providing accommodations and specialized support, educators can create a nurturing and inclusive environment for these children to thrive academically and socially.

In conclusion, collaborative care is essential for ensuring optimal results for children with ASD and ADHD. By harnessing the power of the gut-brain connection and working together, healthcare professionals, educators, therapists, and parents can provide a holistic and comprehensive approach to treatment and support. Through collaborative care, we can unlock the potential within every child and help them lead fulfilling lives.

Multidisciplinary Approach to Autism Spectrum Disorder

In recent years, there has been a growing recognition of the importance of taking a multidisciplinary approach to understanding and treating Autism Spectrum Disorder (ASD). This approach recognizes that ASD is a complex neurodevelopmental disorder that affects not only the brain but also various other systems in the body, including the gut.

The gut-brain connection has emerged as a significant area of research, particularly in relation to children with ASD and ADHD. It is now widely acknowledged that there is a bidirectional communication between the gut and the brain, with each influencing the other's function. This connection has profound implications for children with ASD and ADHD, as it can impact their behavior, cognition, and overall well-being.

One of the key aspects of the multidisciplinary approach to ASD and ADHD is recognizing the role of the gut in these conditions. Research has shown that children with ASD often experience gastrointestinal symptoms such as constipation, diarrhea, and abdominal pain. These symptoms may be related to imbalances in the gut microbiota, which are the trillions of bacteria that reside in the digestive tract. Emerging evidence suggests that these imbalances in gut bacteria may contribute to the development and persistence of ASD and ADHD symptoms.

To address the gut-brain connection in children with ASD and ADHD, a multidisciplinary approach involves collaboration between healthcare professionals from various disciplines, including pediatrics, gastroenterology, neurology, and psychology. By working together, these professionals can develop individualized treatment plans that target both the brain and the gut.

The treatment strategies may include dietary interventions, such as the use of specialized diets like gluten-free and casein-free diets, which have shown promising results in improving ASD and ADHD symptoms. Additionally, probiotics and other interventions aimed at modulating the gut microbiota may also be recommended.

Furthermore, behavioral and educational interventions are essential components of the multidisciplinary approach. These interventions aim to improve social communication skills, reduce challenging behaviors, and enhance overall functioning in children with ASD and ADHD.

It is important for children with ASD and ADHD, as well as their families, to understand the significance of the gut-brain connection and the benefits of a multidisciplinary approach. By addressing both the brain and the gut, healthcare professionals can provide comprehensive care that improves the quality of life for these children. Through ongoing research and collaboration, the understanding of the gut-brain connection will continue to evolve, leading to more effective treatments and interventions for children with ASD and ADHD.

Collaborative Care for Children with ADHD

Children with ADHD often face unique challenges in their daily lives, requiring a collaborative approach to their care. This subchapter focuses on the importance of the gut-brain connection in understanding and managing ADHD symptoms in children. By exploring the gut-brain connection, parents, caregivers, and healthcare professionals can work together to develop effective strategies for supporting children with ADHD and improving their overall well-being.

The gut-brain connection refers to the bidirectional communication between the gut and the brain, which influences various aspects of our physical and mental health. Emerging research suggests that imbalances in the gut microbiome, the community of microorganisms residing in our digestive tract, can contribute to the development and severity of ADHD symptoms in children. Understanding this connection opens up new avenues for intervention and treatment.

Collaborative care begins at home, where parents play a crucial role in supporting their child's overall health. By focusing on nutrition and gut health, parents can make a significant impact on their child's ADHD symptoms. A diet rich in whole foods, high in fiber, and low in processed sugars can help maintain a healthy gut microbiome and support optimal brain function. Additionally, incorporating probiotic-rich foods, such as yogurt and fermented vegetables, can further enhance gut health and potentially reduce ADHD symptoms.

Collaboration extends beyond the home and into the healthcare setting. Pediatricians, psychiatrists, and other healthcare professionals can work together to develop personalized treatment plans for children with ADHD. This may involve a combination of behavioral therapy, medication, and complementary and alternative therapies, such as dietary interventions and supplementation. By considering the gut-brain connection, healthcare professionals can tailor treatments to address the individual needs of each child, leading to more effective outcomes.

Furthermore, collaboration among parents, caregivers, and educators is essential for creating a supportive environment for children with ADHD. By sharing knowledge and strategies, parents can advocate for their child's needs in school and ensure they receive appropriate accommodations and support. Educators can implement classroom strategies that promote focus, attention, and self-regulation, creating a positive learning environment for all children.

In conclusion, understanding the gut-brain connection is crucial for collaborative care in children with ADHD. By focusing on nutrition, personalized treatment plans, and creating a supportive environment, parents, caregivers, healthcare professionals, and educators can work together to improve the overall well-being of children with ADHD. This collaborative approach empowers children to reach their full potential and thrive despite the challenges they may face.

Chapter 6: Nurturing the Gut-Brain Connection for Lifelong Health

Long-Term Implications of a Healthy Gut-Brain Connection

Understanding the long-term implications of a healthy gut-brain connection is crucial for children with ADHD and autism spectrum disorder (ASD). This subchapter delves into the significance of nurturing a strong gut-brain connection and how it can positively impact their lives.

For children with ASD, a well-functioning gut-brain connection can lead to improved cognitive function, communication skills, and behavior. Research has shown that a healthy gut microbiome positively influences brain development, resulting in enhanced social interactions, reduced repetitive behaviors, and improved attention span. By focusing on nurturing their gut health, children with ASD can experience long-term benefits that positively impact their everyday lives.

Similarly, children with ADHD can greatly benefit from a healthy gut-brain connection. Studies have suggested that an imbalanced gut microbiome may contribute to the symptoms of ADHD, such as hyperactivity, impulsivity, and difficulty with focus. By prioritizing gut health, children with ADHD can potentially experience reduced symptoms, increased attention span, and improved impulse control, leading to enhanced academic performance and social interactions.

The long-term implications of a healthy gut-brain connection extend beyond immediate symptom management. By addressing gut health, children with ADHD and ASD may experience improved overall well-being, reduced risk of developing co-occurring conditions, and enhanced quality of life. Additionally, a healthy gut-brain connection has the potential to promote better sleep patterns, which are essential for cognitive function, mood regulation, and overall health.

Nurturing a healthy gut-brain connection involves a multifaceted approach. Implementing a balanced diet that includes probiotic-rich foods, such as yogurt and fermented vegetables, can promote a diverse gut microbiome. Additionally, reducing sugar and processed food intake can help maintain a healthy gut environment. Regular exercise, stress management techniques, and sufficient sleep also play a crucial role in supporting the gut-brain connection.

By understanding the long-term implications of a healthy gut-brain connection, children with ADHD and autism spectrum disorder can take proactive steps towards improving their overall well-being. By prioritizing gut health, they have the potential to experience improved cognitive function, enhanced social interactions, and reduced symptoms. This subchapter aims to empower children with ADHD and autism to take control of their gut health and ultimately lead happier, healthier lives.

Enhancing Cognitive Function and Emotional Well-being

In this subchapter, we will delve into the fascinating topic of enhancing cognitive function and emotional well-being in children with ADHD and Autism Spectrum Disorder (ASD) through the gut-brain connection. The gut-brain connection has emerged as a powerful tool for understanding and addressing the unique challenges faced by these children, offering hope and possibilities for improved quality of life.

Children with Autism Spectrum Disorder often struggle with cognitive functions such as attention, memory, and problem-solving. Similarly, children with ADHD face challenges in focusing, impulsivity, and hyperactivity. The gut-brain connection provides a new lens through which we can explore the underlying causes and potential solutions for these difficulties.

Research has shown that the gut microbiota, the community of microorganisms residing in our digestive system, plays a crucial role in brain development, behavior, and mental health. Imbalances in the gut microbiota, known as dysbiosis, have been found to be more prevalent in children with ASD and ADHD. These imbalances can lead to inflammation, altered neurotransmitter levels, and impaired communication between the gut and the brain.

Fortunately, there are several ways we can enhance cognitive function and emotional well-being by targeting the gut-brain connection. One of the most effective approaches is through dietary interventions. By adopting a gut-friendly diet, rich in prebiotic and probiotic foods, we can promote the growth of beneficial gut bacteria and reduce inflammation. This, in turn, can positively impact cognitive function and emotional regulation.

In addition to dietary changes, other interventions such as gut-healing protocols, targeted supplementation, and behavioral therapies can also support the gut-brain connection. These interventions aim to repair the gut lining, reduce inflammation, and restore balance to the gut microbiota.

Furthermore, lifestyle factors, such as regular exercise, adequate sleep, and stress management, can also play a crucial role in optimizing cognitive function and emotional well-being. Engaging in physical activities, getting enough rest, and practicing relaxation techniques can positively influence the gut-brain axis, leading to improved attention, mood, and overall functioning.

Understanding and harnessing the power of the gut-brain connection offers promising opportunities for children with ADHD and Autism Spectrum Disorder. By exploring the various ways to enhance cognitive function and emotional well-being, we can empower these children to reach their full potential. Through dietary, lifestyle, and therapeutic interventions, we can provide them with the tools they need to thrive and lead fulfilling lives.

Promoting Overall Health and Quality of Life

In this subchapter, we will delve into the importance of promoting overall health and quality of life for children with ADHD and Autism. The gut-brain connection plays a significant role in the well-being of these children, and understanding how to nourish and support this connection can greatly improve their symptoms and overall quality of life.

The gut-brain connection refers to the intricate communication network between the gastrointestinal system and the brain. Research has shown that children with Autism Spectrum Disorder (ASD) and ADHD often have imbalances in their gut microbiome, which can contribute to their symptoms. By addressing these imbalances and promoting a healthy gut, we can positively impact their neurological and behavioral challenges.

One of the key ways to promote overall health is through proper nutrition. A diet rich in whole, unprocessed foods can provide the necessary nutrients for optimal brain function. Incorporating foods that support gut health, such as probiotics and prebiotics, can help restore balance to the gut microbiome. This can be achieved through the inclusion of fermented foods like yogurt, sauerkraut, and kefir, as well as fiber-rich foods like fruits, vegetables, and whole grains.

Physical activity also plays a crucial role in promoting overall health and quality of life. Exercise has been shown to have a positive impact on neurotransmitter levels in the brain, which can help improve attention, mood, and behavior in children with ADHD and Autism. Encouraging regular physical activity, whether through organized sports, outdoor play, or structured exercise routines, can greatly enhance their overall well-being.

Furthermore, promoting good sleep hygiene is essential for children with ADHD and Autism. Poor sleep can exacerbate their symptoms and affect their overall quality of life. Establishing a consistent sleep routine, creating a calm and soothing sleep environment, and minimizing screen time before bed can greatly improve their sleep patterns and overall health.

In conclusion, promoting overall health and quality of life is vital for children with ADHD and Autism. By understanding the gut-brain connection and implementing strategies to support it, we can positively impact their symptoms and enhance their well-being. Through proper nutrition, regular physical activity, and optimizing sleep patterns, we can empower these children to thrive and reach their full potential.

Parental Support and Advocacy

As a parent of a child with ADHD or autism, you play a crucial role in supporting and advocating for your child's well-being and development. Understanding the gut-brain connection can empower you to make informed decisions that can positively impact your child's health and behavior.

The gut-brain connection refers to the bidirectional communication between the brain and the gut. Recent research has shown that the health of the gut can significantly influence brain function and behavior, particularly in children with autism spectrum disorder (ASD) and attention deficit hyperactivity disorder (ADHD). By understanding and addressing this connection, parents can enhance their child's overall well-being.

One of the most important ways parents can support their child is by ensuring a healthy diet. Certain foods, such as those high in sugar, artificial additives, and processed ingredients, can exacerbate symptoms of ADHD and autism. By providing your child with a balanced diet rich in nutrients, such as fruits, vegetables, whole grains, and lean proteins, you can support their gut health and promote optimal brain function.

In addition to diet, parents can also explore supplements and probiotics that support gut health. Probiotics are beneficial bacteria that can help restore and maintain a healthy gut microbiome, which is essential for overall health. Discussing appropriate supplements with your child's healthcare provider can help determine which ones may be beneficial for their specific needs.

Advocacy is another crucial aspect of parental support. It involves being your child's voice and ensuring they receive appropriate accommodations and resources. This may include advocating for educational support, therapies, and access to healthcare professionals who understand the gut-brain connection and its implications for children with ADHD and autism.

Educating yourself about the gut-brain connection is vital to effectively advocate for your child. Research and stay up-to-date with the latest findings, attend workshops or support groups, and connect with other parents who have similar experiences. The more knowledge and support you have, the better equipped you will be to navigate your child's journey.

Remember, you are not alone in this journey. Reach out to other parents, healthcare professionals, and organizations specializing in the gut-brain connection for support and guidance. With your unwavering support and advocacy, your child can thrive and lead a fulfilling life.

Empowering Parents with Knowledge and Resources

Parents play an integral role in the lives of children with ADHD and Autism Spectrum Disorder (ASD). They are the primary caregivers, advocates, and support systems for their children. Empowering parents with knowledge and resources is crucial in helping them navigate the challenges that come with raising a child with these conditions.

Understanding the Gut-Brain Connection for Kids with Autism Spectrum Disorder

One aspect that parents should be aware of is the Gut-Brain Connection for Kids with Autism Spectrum Disorder. Research has shown that there is a strong link between the gut and the brain, and imbalances in the gut microbiome can contribute to the development and severity of ASD symptoms. By understanding this connection, parents can take proactive steps to improve their child's gut health, which in turn may positively impact their behavior, cognition, and overall well-being.

Providing parents with information on the Gut-Brain Connection will enable them to make informed decisions about their child's diet and lifestyle. They can learn about the importance of a balanced and nutritious diet, as well as the potential benefits of incorporating probiotics and prebiotics into their child's daily routine. Moreover, parents can also explore the potential benefits of certain dietary interventions, such as gluten-free or casein-free diets, which have shown promising results in some children with ASD.

Unlocking the Gut-Brain Connection for Kids with ADHD

Similarly, parents of children with ADHD can benefit from understanding the Gut-Brain Connection specific to their child's condition. While the exact cause of ADHD remains unknown, recent studies have highlighted the role of gut health in the manifestation of ADHD symptoms. By gaining knowledge about this connection, parents can adopt strategies to support their child's gut health and potentially alleviate some of the symptoms associated with ADHD.

Parents can learn about the importance of a balanced diet rich in fruits, vegetables, and whole grains, as well as the potential benefits of omega-3 fatty acids found in fish oil supplements. Additionally, they can explore the impact of food additives, such as artificial colors and preservatives, on their child's behavior and consider reducing their consumption. By providing parents with this information, they can make informed choices when it comes to their child's nutrition and overall well-being.

Equipping parents with resources

In addition to knowledge, parents need access to resources that can support them on their journey. From support groups and online forums to books and reputable websites, there are numerous avenues for parents to connect with others facing similar challenges and gain insights from experts in the field.

These resources can provide a sense of community, guidance, and emotional support, empowering parents to advocate for their child's needs effectively.

Conclusion

Empowering parents with knowledge and resources is essential in helping them support their children with ADHD and Autism Spectrum Disorder. By understanding the Gut-Brain Connection and having access to relevant resources, parents can make informed decisions about their child's diet, lifestyle, and overall well-being. With this knowledge, parents can become effective advocates, providing their children with the best possible care and support.

Advocating for Improved Gut-Brain Health in Education and Healthcare Systems

In recent years, there has been an increasing recognition of the profound impact that the gut-brain connection has on the well-being of children with Autism Spectrum Disorder (ASD) and Attention Deficit Hyperactivity Disorder (ADHD). This subchapter aims to shed light on the importance of advocating for improved gut-brain health within the education and healthcare systems, specifically tailored to the needs of children with ASD and ADHD.

The gut-brain connection refers to the bidirectional communication between the gut and the brain, facilitated by the intricate network of neurons and chemicals. Research has shown that disruptions in this connection can contribute to the development and exacerbation of neurodevelopmental disorders such as ASD and ADHD. Therefore, it is crucial that educational and healthcare institutions prioritize understanding and addressing these underlying gut-brain issues.

One key area for improvement is in the education system. Teachers and school administrators need to be equipped with knowledge about the gut-brain connection and its impact on children with ASD and ADHD. This understanding can help them create supportive environments that promote optimal gut-brain health. Strategies such as implementing sensory-friendly classrooms, providing nutritious meals, and incorporating regular physical activity can all contribute to improved overall well-being.

Furthermore, healthcare systems must also play a pivotal role in advocating for improved gut-brain health. Medical professionals need to recognize the importance of addressing gut health as part of the treatment plan for children with ASD and ADHD. This may involve working closely with nutritionists and dieticians to create personalized dietary plans that support gut health and reduce inflammation. Additionally, healthcare providers should be open to exploring alternative treatment options like probiotics and gut-healing supplements, which have shown promise in improving symptoms associated with these disorders.

Advocacy from parents and caregivers is also crucial in bringing about positive change. By sharing their experiences and knowledge about the gut-brain connection, they can raise awareness within their communities, schools, and healthcare settings. This can lead to increased support and resources for children with ASD and ADHD, ultimately improving their quality of life.

In conclusion, advocating for improved gut-brain health within the education and healthcare systems is vital for children with ASD and ADHD. By prioritizing this aspect, we can create a more inclusive and supportive environment that recognizes the unique needs of these children. With increased awareness, knowledge, and collaboration, we can pave the way for better outcomes and brighter futures for children with ASD and ADHD.

Future Directions in Gut-Brain Connection Research

As we continue to learn more about the gut-brain connection, exciting new avenues for research are emerging that could greatly benefit children with Autism Spectrum Disorder (ASD) and Attention Deficit Hyperactivity

Disorder (ADHD). Scientists and medical professionals are dedicated to unraveling the mysteries of this complex relationship to develop effective treatments and interventions for children like you.

One future direction in gut-brain connection research is exploring the role of the gut microbiome in neurodevelopmental disorders. The gut microbiome refers to the trillions of microorganisms that reside in your digestive system. Recent studies have shown that the composition of these microorganisms can affect brain development and function. By studying the specific bacteria present in the gut of children with ASD and ADHD, researchers hope to identify patterns and understand how they may influence symptoms.

Another promising avenue of research involves investigating the impact of diet on the gut-brain connection. Certain foods and nutrients have been shown to have a direct effect on brain function and behavior. Scientists are studying how different diets, such as a gluten-free or dairy-free diet, may alleviate symptoms in children with ASD and ADHD. By identifying specific dietary interventions, we may be able to provide children like you with personalized nutrition plans to support your cognitive and emotional well-being.

Furthermore, researchers are exploring the potential of probiotics and prebiotics to improve gut health and alleviate symptoms of neurodevelopmental disorders. Probiotics are beneficial bacteria that can be consumed through foods or supplements, while prebiotics are dietary fibers that promote the growth of beneficial bacteria. By targeting the gut microbiome with these interventions, scientists hope to restore balance and optimize brain function.

Additionally, advancements in technology, such as neuroimaging and genetic analysis, are allowing researchers to gain a deeper understanding of the gut-brain connection. These tools enable scientists to study the intricate interactions between the gut and the brain at a molecular level. By uncovering the underlying mechanisms, we can develop more targeted therapies and interventions to help children with ASD and ADHD.

In conclusion, the future of gut-brain connection research holds great promise for children with Autism Spectrum Disorder and Attention Deficit Hyperactivity Disorder. The exploration of the gut microbiome, dietary interventions, probiotics and prebiotics, as well as advancements in technology, will provide us with valuable insights into this intricate relationship. By understanding and harnessing the power of the gut-brain connection, we can develop effective treatments and interventions to support your overall well-being and help you thrive.

Advancements in Gut Microbiome Research

In recent years, there have been groundbreaking advancements in the field of gut microbiome research. Scientists have discovered that the gut plays a crucial role in the overall health and well-being of individuals, especially children with Autism Spectrum Disorder (ASD) and Attention Deficit Hyperactivity Disorder (ADHD). This subchapter aims to explore the latest findings and developments in gut-brain connection research, specifically tailored to children with ADHD and autism.

The gut microbiome refers to the trillions of microorganisms residing in our digestive tract. These microorganisms, including bacteria, viruses, and fungi, work together to maintain a healthy balance in our bodies. Recent studies have shown that the gut microbiome has a direct impact on brain function and behavior, with disruptions in its composition linked to neurological disorders such as ASD and ADHD.

One significant advancement in gut microbiome research is the identification of specific microbial strains that can positively influence brain health. Researchers have discovered that certain beneficial bacteria, such as Bifidobacterium and Lactobacillus, can help regulate brain activity and improve cognitive function. These findings have paved the way for the development of probiotics and prebiotics, which are dietary supplements that aim to restore a healthy gut microbiome.

Moreover, scientists have begun exploring the role of diet in modulating the gut-brain connection. Certain foods, such as those high in fiber and omega-3 fatty acids, have been found to promote a diverse and healthy gut microbiome, leading to improved cognitive abilities and reduced behavioral symptoms. This research has provided valuable insights into the importance of nutrition in managing ADHD and autism symptoms.

Furthermore, advancements in gut microbiome research have also shed light on the potential of fecal microbiota transplantation (FMT) as a treatment option for children with ASD and ADHD. FMT involves the transfer of fecal matter from a healthy donor to the recipient's gut, aiming to restore a healthy microbial balance. Although this therapy is still in its early stages, initial studies have shown promising results in alleviating symptoms and improving overall well-being.

In conclusion, the advancements in gut microbiome research have revolutionized our understanding of the gut-brain connection, particularly in children with ADHD and autism. The identification of beneficial bacteria, the role of diet, and the potential of FMT as a treatment option have opened up new possibilities for managing and improving the lives of children with these conditions. As researchers continue to delve into this fascinating field, we can expect further advancements that will continue to shape the future of gut-brain connection research and its applications in neurodevelopmental disorders.

Potential Therapeutic Interventions for Autism and ADHD

When it comes to addressing the challenges of autism and ADHD, it is important to consider the potential therapeutic interventions that can make a positive impact on the lives of children with these conditions. The gut-brain connection has emerged as a promising avenue for understanding and treating these neurodevelopmental disorders.

For children with Autism Spectrum Disorder (ASD), therapeutic interventions that focus on the gut-brain connection can help to alleviate symptoms and enhance overall well-being. One such intervention is dietary modifications. Research has shown that certain foods can exacerbate symptoms of autism, while others can improve them. A diet low in gluten and casein, for example, has been found to be beneficial for many children with ASD. Similarly, probiotics and prebiotics can promote a healthy balance of gut bacteria, which has been linked to improved behavior and cognitive function.

In the case of ADHD, interventions that target the gut-brain connection can also have a significant impact. Studies have shown that omega-3 fatty acids, found in fish oil supplements, can reduce hyperactivity and impulsivity in children with ADHD. Additionally, certain diets that focus on eliminating artificial additives and food colorings have been found to improve attention and reduce symptoms of ADHD.

Another potential therapeutic intervention for both autism and ADHD is gut microbiota transplantation. This procedure involves transferring healthy gut bacteria from a donor to a recipient, with the aim of restoring a healthy balance of gut bacteria. Preliminary studies have shown promising results, with improvements in behavior and cognitive function observed in children with ASD and ADHD.

Furthermore, mindfulness-based interventions have been found to be effective in managing symptoms of both autism and ADHD. Techniques such as meditation and deep breathing exercises can help children develop self-regulation skills, reduce anxiety, and improve attention and focus.

It is important to note that while these interventions show promise, they may not work for every child. Each individual is unique, and it is essential to work closely with healthcare professionals to develop an individualized treatment plan that takes into account the specific needs and preferences of the child.

In conclusion, the gut-brain connection offers a range of potential therapeutic interventions for children with autism and ADHD. From dietary modifications to gut microbiota transplantation and mindfulness-based interventions, there are various strategies that can help improve symptoms and enhance overall well-being. By understanding and harnessing the power of the gut-brain connection, we can provide children with autism and ADHD with the support they need to thrive.

Conclusion: Embracing the Power of the Gut-Brain Connection

In this book, "The Amazing Gut-Brain Connection: How it Helps Kids with Autism and ADHD," we have explored the fascinating link between our gut and brain and how it can positively impact children with Autism Spectrum Disorder (ASD) and Attention Deficit Hyperactivity Disorder (ADHD). Throughout these pages, we have discovered the remarkable potential of this connection and how it can improve the lives of children who face these challenges.

The gut-brain connection is a complex network of communication between our gut, where millions of bacteria reside, and our brain. This connection plays a crucial role in regulating our mood, behavior, and cognitive function. For children with ASD and ADHD, strengthening this connection can lead to significant improvements in their overall well-being.

Research has shown that a healthy gut contributes to a healthy brain. By nurturing a balanced gut microbiome through proper nutrition, children can experience reduced symptoms of hyperactivity, impulsivity, and inattention. Incorporating a diet rich in probiotics, prebiotics, and fiber can promote the growth of beneficial bacteria in the gut, improving cognitive function and reducing anxiety and irritability.

Furthermore, understanding the gut-brain connection allows parents and caregivers to make informed decisions about their child's health. By recognizing the impact of certain foods on behavior and mood, they can make dietary adjustments that support emotional regulation and focus.

In embracing the power of the gut-brain connection, we empower children with ASD and ADHD to take control of their own well-being. By making small lifestyle changes, such as practicing regular exercise, getting enough sleep, and managing stress, they can optimize their gut health and enhance their brain function.

It is important to note that the gut-brain connection is still an emerging field of study, and more research is needed. However, the evidence gathered so far suggests that there is a significant link between gut health and neurodevelopmental disorders. By raising awareness about this connection, we hope to inspire further investigation and understanding in the scientific community.

In conclusion, the gut-brain connection holds immense potential for children with Autism Spectrum Disorder and Attention Deficit Hyperactivity Disorder. By nurturing a healthy gut, we can positively impact their cognitive function, behavior, and overall well-being. Let us embrace the power of this connection and continue to explore its possibilities for the benefit of all children with ASD and ADHD.